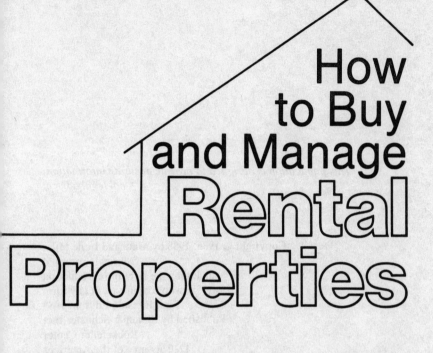

How to Buy and Manage Rental Properties

MIKE and IRENE MILIN

A FIRESIDE BOOK
PUBLISHED BY SIMON & SCHUSTER
NEW YORK   LONDON   TORONTO   SYDNEY   TOKYO   SINGAPORE

*This publication is designed to provide accurate information,
not legal advice.*

Designed by Irving Perkins Associates
Manufactured in the United States of America

24 25 26 27 28 29 30

Library of Congress Cataloging in Publication Data
Milin, Mike.
How to buy and manage rental properties.

Includes index.
1. Apartment houses—Purchasing.   2. Apartment houses—
Management.   3. Garden apartments.   4. Landlord and tenant.
5. Real estate management.   I. Milin, Irene.   II. Title.
HD1394.M55   1986   647'.92'068   86-6454
ISBN 0-671-60701-4
ISBN 0-671-64423-8 Pbk.

Acknowledgments

SPECIAL THANKS GO to our friend, Dave Chodack, for his invaluable assistance in the creation of this book.

WE ARE ALSO GRATEFUL to all our real estate seminar teachers, who opened up the world of real estate opportunities and provided us with inspiration and knowledge, and to all of the other terrific people who inspired and motivated us through books, tapes, and by personal example.

To the thousands of people successfully using "The Milin Method," changing their lives and inspiring us to forge ahead,

And to the countless others who yearn for financial independence, are endowed with the entrepreneurial spirit, but lack the cash, credit or knowledge, we dedicate this book. To these future millionaires, we contribute the proven know-how to help you achieve *your* dreams. This is the only country in the world where you can still start off broke and end up a millionaire. We know, because we've done it!

Contents

Introduction

Real estate investing works if you do. It's one of the simplest and safest ways for the average person to get rich today. We know, because we've done it and it didn't even take us very long. We're barely into our thirties and we've already got more than enough money to live comfortably for the rest of our lives. And we owe it all to real estate.

Just a few years ago, we were broke and in debt. We were at a crossroads in life. We both had college degrees, but all they got us were periodic bouts of unemployment, a series of dead-end jobs, and a growing stack of unpaid bills.

WORKING FOR OTHERS DOESN'T WORK

Finally we came to the firm conclusion that working for others was *not* the solution. Clearly, we were on an endless treadmill and drastic changes were needed. Then, one day, we saw an ad for a real estate seminar by Dr. Albert J. Lowry, who claimed to be a self-made millionaire.

We were desperate at this point, so we decided to take a chance. We suddenly thought about all the famous Americans who had become wealthy by investing in real estate—from George Washington to William Zeckendorf—and we got the heady idea of following in their footsteps.

We decided to invest in ourselves by learning how to invest in real estate. We didn't have any money, but we did have credit cards, so we charged the seminar fee on our Mastercard. Of course, we didn't know how we were going to pay the bill at that point, but we knew that we had at least thirty days to worry about it and then we could just pay the minimum due each month until it was paid off.

That seminar proved to be the turning point in our lives. It gave us the information we needed to get started and left us hungry for more. We spent the next six months living from hand to mouth and poured every cent into books, tapes, and seminar fees.

THREE YEARS TO FREEDOM

We read everything we could get our hands on and attended every seminar and investment group meeting we could find. Then we went out knocking on doors, talking to property owners, and making offers. We were determined to learn enough to turn our lives around and that's just what we did.

We borrowed money from a friend so we could move from the San Francisco area, where we had been living for the past few years, to Tucson, Arizona. We felt there were more opportunities in the Southwest and we wanted to make a fresh start.

That was four years ago. Today, we live in a custom house in the most exclusive area of town and control and manage a portfolio of about one hundred single-family houses and small income properties worth about $12 million. Instead of sitting around managing those properties the usual labor-intensive way, we spend our time playing with our daughter, Tanya, and cruising to exotic islands in the sun, when we're not out looking for new real estate deals.

Real estate investing not only opened the door to financial independence, it now also provides an ideal opportunity for us to live and work together as a team. Because it provides us with a life-style that balances work and play, and the opportunity to travel and to meet interesting people from all walks of life, we get a lot more out of it than just a lot of money.

We took a little bit from each person, each book, and each seminar and blended it all into a system of our own. We did a lot of unorthodox things and took some chances, but it paid off. Within nine months after we started, we controlled more than seventy-five single-family houses and word of our success seemed to spread like wildfire. Soon other people were seeking us out, wanting to know our secrets, asking *us* to teach seminars. Because we can reach only a limited number of people that way, we decided to write this book. Anybody can do what we did if he follows the system we lay out in this book. It truly makes landlording easy, and landlording is one of the quickest paths to wealth. Sure, there are other ways to get rich, but being a landlord is the safest and the most accessible to the average person.

LANDLORDING IS THE WORLD'S MOST PROFITABLE BUSINESS

In almost any community, anywhere in the world, the richest people are almost invariably the landlords, the people who own property and rent it out to others. Landlording is probably the world's second oldest profession and certainly the most lucrative. Properly managed, a good piece of income property is the closest thing you will ever find to a real live, self-propelled, self-generating money machine.

TWO REASONS WHY PEOPLE ARE SCARED TO BUY REAL ESTATE

If it's so easy to make money by owning income property, why aren't more people landlords? Why is it that the average person shies away from getting involved in real estate? There are countless excuses, but the most common reasons given are these:

1. *Lack of Knowledge.* Ignorance is probably the greatest deterrent. People need to know how to get started, how to buy right, and how to finance real estate with little or no money down. We cover all those points in this book.

2. *Fear of Property Management.* Tenants are the second major reason why people are afraid to become real estate investors. They've heard all the horror stories about late rent, late-night complaints, vandalism, problems with evictions, and all the other bad things that can come with owning income prop-

erty. They are afraid they won't be able to handle it all. So were we, until we developed our own hands-off formula for keeping tenants happy and well-behaved.

While there are many fine books on purchasing real estate, this book is meant to help:

• beginners getting started in buying and managing real estate
• small investors with one- to four-unit properties who have experienced management problems

This book is the road map to guide you to your financial goals. It can be a valuable aid for those who seek a reprieve from the treadmill of a job, the enslavement of a career or profession they are not really happy with, or those who just want to improve their investment portfolio. It is an action plan for you to follow, step-by-step, and it is based on our own successful rags-to-riches experience with real estate investing.

SUCCESSFUL MANAGEMENT MEANS SUCCESSFUL INVESTING

It's not just buying property that assures financial success. It's the way you manage the property that provides the cash flow that leads to financial independence. We'll show you how to take your properties and put them on an "automatic pilot" system by mastering the simple principle "Manage people, not property." We'll show you how:

• to keep the property rented (no vacancies)
• to attract good tenants, and keep them
• to obtain the most rent
• to ensure the rent is paid on time
• to involve tenants effectively in keeping expenses down, and in the self-management of the property

A "HANDS-OFF" CASH-FLOW MANAGEMENT PLAN

The goal of owning real estate is to become financially independent. It is *not* to create a burdensome job of property management. By using a "hands-off" approach, as we have done, it is possible to have the actual property management provide the cash flow that allows you to become financially independent.

Each year, the income from the property should grow, while the expenses remain relatively fixed. Then, eventually, you will pay off any loans outstanding and your expenses will shrink to almost nothing. Your only expense will be property taxes while the income continues to grow. Then, your biggest problem will be what to do with all your cash flow. Many successful landlords find that after five to ten years, the money is literally coming in faster than they can spend it. They have to keep opening new bank accounts just to stay below the $100,000 per account limit for insured savings. And many of them earned this income in their spare time.

You *can* do it yourself, as the two of us have done, because you *are* the one best motivated to watch your own investment interests.

LANDLORDING STILL HAS A BAD IMAGE

Bad landlords have given all landlords a bad image. Landlords are often depicted as heartless money grubbers who would trade their mothers for a rent increase, or else as overworked, underpaid drudges, who end up as slaves to their properties and their tenants. No matter which side they're on, most people just assume that all landlords hate dealing with their tenants and that all tenants automatically hate their landlord. This is because far too many landlords have no idea how to manage rental property. Ignorance breeds inefficiency, and these bad landlords make life miserable for everyone. When it's badly managed, real estate is not just another wasted resource; it becomes an active drain on all your other resources: your time, your energy, your money. It can make you sorry that you didn't just take your money (even if you bought the property for no money down) and put it in the bank. Good management is the key to everything.

OWNING RENTAL PROPERTY DOESN'T HAVE TO BE HARD WORK

We believe that landlording is a serious business, but there's no reason why it has to be a job. If you do it right, it should not take more than one or two days a month, no matter how many properties you own. You need to go to the post office to collect your mail on the first of each month and you will occasionally have to interview new tenants. Otherwise, you shouldn't be involved. We have over two hundred properties, but we're almost never home anymore. We're always on the road, lecturing and teaching seminars and workshops. We don't have time for filling frequent vacancies, chasing down tenants who pay their rent late or not at all, or fixing leaky faucets and replacing light bulbs and washers.

THE MANAGEMENT BURDEN IS ON THE TENANTS

Therefore, we've worked out a system that eliminates most of these problems. We have our own management company now, with a full-time property manager whom we trained. But no one person can handle one hundred properties all alone, so we put most of the burden on the tenants.

Some people feel guilty when their lives are too easy. If they own rental property and they are making money without putting in too much effort, they get uncomfortable and feel as if they haven't earned their money. They feel compelled to constantly ride herd on their tenants and/or their resident and nonresident managers and make their properties the main focus of their lives. We don't.

How to Buy and Manage Rental Properties takes the pain out of managing property. It's a better way of doing things for both the beginner and the experienced property owner. It's based on three simple principles:

- making money when you buy the property
- making money while you own the property, and
- making money when you sell the property.

In order to do this, you don't manage the property, you manage people: buyers, sellers, and, most of all, tenants. You buy the right properties, the ones that will attract the right tenants, and then you sit back and let them manage themselves.

There are other management books available, but they're aimed primarily at owners of large apartment complexes with resident and/or professional managers. After all, the bigger the building, the more money you can make. And if you use hired management, you don't even have to get involved with your properties at all. You can be an absentee owner. While that approach has its definite advantages, this book is aimed at the do-it-yourself owner-manager.

We feel that one of the big advantages to investing in real estate is that you have control over your money. If we wanted to be passive investors, we would put our money in the stock market, or into gold or other commodities. We don't want to be passive investors, but we don't want to be full-time landlords, either, so we buy easy-to-manage single-family houses and small income properties of five units or less. Now let's see how the program works.

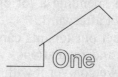
One

Successful Landlording Is No Accident

Being a successful landlord doesn't require a lot of hard work, but it does require planning. For every hour you spend before you buy the property and/or rent it to someone, you will save ten hours later. There are certain simple steps to follow that will make the job easier, and we'll go through them in the course of this book, devoting a chapter to each one, from picking the right properties to getting the best possible price and terms when you sell.

THE RIGHT PROPERTY ATTRACTS THE RIGHT TENANTS

You can't go fishing without the right bait. Everyone knows that. And the right bait to attract the tenants you want is the right kind of property. Put yourself in the tenants' position and ask yourself what you would look for. You want tenants who want to be upwardly mobile and you want them to feel that renting from you is a step up, a step in the right direction. Therefore, you have to buy property with the future tenants in mind.

Our tenants are resident managers who work practically for free. They clean the properties they live in, they paint, and they even add patios, decks, and porches at their own expense. They do all this because they think of our properties as their homes. We encourage them to feel this way and we pick the kind of people who like to work on their homes and improve them. We believe in spending a lot of time and effort before we rent to people, not afterward.

We select our tenants carefully and then we patiently explain our rules and regulations. We have an eleven-page rental contract and we go over it with prospective tenants line by line. We spend an average of an hour and a half going through the rental agreement with prospective tenants and we have them initial every page. This way, there are no misunderstandings later.

Renting from us is a special privilege; we don't rent to just anyone. We look for a certain type of tenant, someone who's looking for a *home,* not just another rental situation. If people are just looking for any place to rent, there are plenty of places out there. If landlords are just looking for any tenants to rent to, there are plenty of them out there, too. We are looking for a special few.

The tenants we want are family-oriented blue-collar workers who would like to buy a house but can't afford it. They rent from us because it's the next best thing.

Don't Buy Rental Property in Rental Areas

The ideal is to buy all your rental property in areas where most residences are owner-occupied. The neighbors may not love this idea, but your tenants will. This is the first principle that you should keep in mind. Everyone wants to step up in the world, not down.

It is said that the three most important things in real estate are location, location, and location, and location is just as important to prospective tenants as it is to buyers. Our tenants prefer to live in areas that are primarily owner-occupied, because they are nicer, more prestigious, and better places to raise their families. If an area is mostly tenant-occupied, there will be a lot of transients and a lot of tenant turnover. It's harder to get to know the neighbors and establish long-term, stable relationships when people are moving in and out all the time. If your tenants are stable family people, this is not what they want for their children or for themselves.

It is not really what you want for yourself, either. Areas that are mostly renter-occupied have higher vacancy rates. If your tenants decide that they're not happy where they are living, they can easily pick up and move. They can meet with other tenants and organize or just compare notes about rents, conditions, and other subjects. This can lead to trouble.

Owner-Occupied Areas Are Stable

Owner-occupied areas have less turnover and lower vacancy rates. They are better places to live in and raise their families. They are also better places to be a landlord.

Better tenants and a lower vacancy rate mean fewer problems. Problems take time and energy that you could use in other ways, such as making money. So this is the first thing to think about when you think about becoming a landlord: where to look for suitable properties and how to find them. You have to decide what you want in a rental property and what type of people you want for tenants. Then you have to actively seek out the types of properties that will appeal to the tenants you want.

How to Buy and Manage Rental Properties is based on this simple principle. We stick to single-family houses and small income properties, because we feel they give us more control. Smaller properties are generally more desirable to live in. They are often located in better areas and they attract a better class of tenants.

It's Hard to Think of One Hundred Units as "Home"

Large apartment buildings and complexes rarely have a homey feeling. The bigger they are, the more impersonal they seem. Unless they have luxury features, such as recreational facilities, the units generally rent for less than comparable units in smaller buildings and attract a different type of tenant. We like family people as tenants, and high-rise complexes are not generally good places for families. They are rarely located in good owner-occupied neighborhoods. When you find one large apartment complex, you generally find a lot of them. Home owners don't want large apartment buildings in their neighborhoods; in fact, large buildings are usually excluded from the better areas by zoning laws.

Rental homes and even small apartment buildings are more desirable because they create less congestion and population density and thus face less opposition. Therefore, they are often found in the better areas, among the owner-occupied single-family homes, where people are eager to rent.

YOU WANT TENANTS WHO ARE EAGER TO RENT FROM YOU

Tenants who really want to rent your place are not likely to give you trouble. Nor are they likely to move as soon as they find a "better" deal somewhere else. We have good relations with our tenants because we do our homework before we rent to them. We find out what people want and then we give it to them at a reasonable price. In return, we insist they maintain the properties in good condition and take care of all minor repairs themselves.

There's nothing really complicated about it. Tenants are people and if you treat them firmly but fairly, they will usually respond in a positive way.

We occasionally make mistakes and we have tenant problems just like anyone else. No matter how carefully you interview people and check their backgrounds, one or two problem types always manage to slip through. We've even had to evict a couple of people when they turned out to be troublemakers and/or deadbeats. But a few bad tenants out of more than one hundred people we've rented to over the last four years is not a bad track record. We know our system works.

There's more to being a successful landlord than finding good properties and choosing good tenants to rent them to. Many people never get their properties rented, because they give up. They get so tired of interviewing tenants and making appointments with people who never show up that they just sell their properties instead—often at a loss.

We don't make appointments with prospective tenants except at our office and at our convenience. We are there anyway. If they don't show up, it's their loss, not ours. But what if you don't have an office? If you have only one or two properties to manage, you definitely don't need an office, but prospective tenants don't have to know that you don't have one.

KEEP TENANTS IN AWE OF YOU

Let your tenants think that they are dealing with a big company, even if you are a one-man operation. If you don't have an office, let them think you do. Let people come to you; never go to them. We have worked out a system for this, too. It's all part of the *How to Buy and Manage Rental Properties* program.

When we started out, we didn't have an office. We worked out of our home, but the tenants never knew that. They were always convinced that they were meeting us at or near our office. It made sense to them that they had to come to us, rather than meeting us at the property.

Once you start meeting tenants at the property, they have the upper hand. They are taking up your time and energy at their convenience. That is no good. You should remain firmly in control at all times. You either want to give prospective tenants the keys and let them look at the property themselves, or else hold the property open for the entire world to see at one time. We have developed methods for doing both of these successfully, so that we waste as little of our time as possible. We don't like vacancies, so when we do get them, we try to fill them quickly and painlessly.

YOU MUST ATTRACT RENTERS BEFORE YOU CAN CHOOSE ONE

That means you've got to advertise. That's part of our program, too. Over the years, we've developed ads that work. They draw the tenants we want and they get the message across simply and economically.

There are many different media: TV, radio, newspapers, and others. No matter which you pick, you've got to let people know you're out there. You can't rent a place that no one knows about, no matter how nice it is. Compare prices in your area and then think about the potential impact that each medium will have on the prospective tenants you want to reach. You'll find sample forms to guide you later in the book.

YOU'VE GOT TO KNOW WHERE THE MONEY'S GOING

Getting the tenants to pay their rent is only half the battle. You have to have records so that you know whether or not they paid and whether or not they paid on time. When you manage as many properties as we do and you're home as little as we are, you have to be able to stay on top of all the details at a glance.

We can't afford to get behind in our bills any more than we can afford to let our tenants get behind in their rent. We have to make sure that all our bills are paid promptly for each property each and every month. Each time we write a check, we have to know what it's for and why. Fortunately, we've discovered an easy system for cross-referencing all the information we need.

THE RIGHT TIME TO SELL YOUR PROPERTIES

Knowing when to sell your properties is vitally important, and we have a system for that, too. We call it tracking the properties, keeping track of how quickly they are appreciating and how quickly the rents are going up. Certain properties are natural winners. The rents just keep going up and the properties keep appreciating. Others need help to reach their full potential, and a third group just aren't worth holding on to. We get rid of them sooner than the others.

KEEPING EXPENSES UNDER CONTROL

Cutting expenses is one way to increase the cash flow and make properties more valuable. We have learned where to put our money to get the maximum effect. We don't like to waste money any more than we like to waste time or effort, so we cut all unnecessary costs.

Little things add up, but not as quickly as big ones. You can increase your cash flow just so much by cutting expenses. For the really big gains, you've got to increase the rents. How do you increase the rents without alienating the tenants and driving them out? That is what every successful landlord needs to know. We have developed letters that we send to our tenants.

We have one letter for the good tenants that we want to keep and another letter for the bad tenants, the ones we want to get rid of. (You'll see copies of these later on.) We start off with rents that are slightly below the average for the areas where our properties are located. This gives good tenants an incentive to move in. If they pay their rent on time, keep up with the maintenance, and follow our other rules, we will keep their rent low. That encourages them to stay.

If they don't do what they're supposed to do, we will raise their rent more often and in bigger increments. If they pay, we make extra profits. If they leave, we get better tenants to replace them. Either way, we come out ahead.

Getting rid of all tenants without losing any income should be every landlord's ultimate dream. It can become a reality with a few simple techniques. We have some properties that we've already sold but still pay us a regular income, just like the ones we are holding as rentals, because we carry loans rather than cashing out. On the other hand, we know people who lost years of hard work and sweat equity when they sold their properties the wrong way, to the wrong people. *We eliminate that problem by showing you how to do it right!*

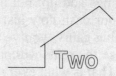

Two

People—Not Properties —Cause Problems

Properties don't cause problems. People do. Buildings just sit there, quietly minding their own business and cranking out money for you. They don't try to abuse you or take advantage of you. Sure, houses and other types of property are quite capable of producing anxiety. Roofs leak, sewer and other plumbing lines break, paint wears out, and lawns need periodic cutting. Then there are fires, floods, blizzards, earthquakes, tornadoes, hurricanes, and all the other possible calamities that can plague property owners.

But all these things are beyond the property owner's control. Tenants are not. Tenants can be controlled and tenants are the main source of real problems property owners encounter.

Think of the traditional worries beginning property owners or would-be property owners think about: not getting the rent on time—or not getting it at all; evictions and other court hassles; tenants who refuse to move even after they have been evicted and who may even damage the property before they do leave; rent control; negative cash flow that they can't handle; tenants who move after a couple of months, creating vacancy problems. . . .

These are all *people* problems. They all stem from the same problem: renting to the wrong people. If you pick the right tenants, these problems can be eliminated.

The big problem that scares people away from real estate and prevents them from getting rich is that they don't know how to choose tenants or manage them. They don't know how to deal with people.

How many people really let the fear of earthquakes, floods, tornadoes, and other disasters keep them from investing in real estate? There may be a few out there, but not many. Most people who give one of those reasons are making excuses. They don't want to admit that they are afraid of dealing with tenants and don't know how to go about it.

Owning and managing rental property is a business, and you have to conduct yourself in a businesslike manner. You have to recognize that running any business involves dealing with people. If all there was to it was dealing with bookkeeping and numbers, there would be a lot more successful businesspeople in the world, and every bookkeeper and accountant busily slaving away for someone else would go into business for himself.

BUSINESS IS PEOPLE

People are the key to running a business. They will be your customers, your employees, and your suppliers. If you know how to work with people and get them to want to work with you, you can be successful in almost any business there is, and this applies more to the rental business than to most others.

Property problems are almost invariably people problems. Apartment buildings do not smash their own windows or doors. They don't draw on the walls, or put holes in the carpets. Nor do houses let their friends park cars and motorcycles on the lawn. They don't get drunk and punch holes in their own walls.

Tenants don't do this, either, unless they think that they can get away with it, or unless they have a deliberate reason to act vindictively toward you. Either way, it is your fault. You did something wrong, or it would not have happened. Either you picked the wrong tenants to begin with, or you handled them wrong once they were in your property. Maybe you were too lenient and easygoing the first few times they did something wrong, and this gave them the idea you were a pushover. Maybe you were a rent gouger, taking advantage of people desperate for a place to live and charging them higher-than-market rents.

Or you could be a slumlord who refuses to stay on top of maintenance and repairs.

If you don't maintain your property, how can you expect the tenants to do it for you? They are going to take their cue from you. If you don't care about the property, they won't either; and if you let them get away with running your property into the ground, they will take advantage of it.

It is your business. You—and not the tenants—are the boss. You are the one who sets the tone. If the business is well run, it will be because you know how to run it smoothly and efficiently and how to communicate this to your tenants *before* they move in. Afterward it may be too late.

Give your tenants a clear set of guidelines and expectations. Let them know what you will do for them as a landlord and what you expect them to do for you. Also let them know what you will *not* do for them. This way, you will avoid setting any false expectations on either side. Be clear with them about what maintenance and repairs you expect them to do and what you will be responsible for. Make sure they understand that they will be expected to meet your standards and that you will check up on them to make sure they are keeping the property up.

In order to make this really effective, you should have a system of rewards and punishments, with the accent on the rewards, to be positive. Expect the most from your tenants and then give them every reason to live up to it.

INVESTING IN TENANTS

With the dramatic increase in the median selling price of a home, fewer and fewer people can afford to buy a home. We are on the verge of becoming a society of long-term renters. Young families used to look forward to renting for a short time and then buying their own homes. Now many of them are resigned to being renters indefinitely.

This gives them a very different perspective. They are looking for a home, not just a place to stop temporarily. These are the tenants you want, because they are stable. They are the ones who will make your rental program work, but only if you train them properly.

That's right. You have to train them. Well-trained tenants can be your best friends. They will be loyal, faithful, and obedient, and will be putting money in your pocket. You can't assume that they know how to be good tenants, so you have to work with them. After all, you want to establish a long-term relationship. Therefore, your tenants are an investment, just as your property is. The more time you put into choosing your tenants and working with them, the more productive they will be.

How do you train your tenants? The methods you use will vary according to the amount of property you own, the type of tenant you are dealing with, and your own personality. If you are buying and renting properties in the poor part of town, where most of your tenants are marginally educated, your approach will be different from what it would be if you were dealing with white-collar workers and professionals. A person who owns three hundred houses will also do things differently than someone who owns only four or five.

What you tell your tenants about how much property you own is also part of the training program. Some landlords want their tenants to know that they are dealing with a large, powerful concern. In many cases, the landlords don't even want the tenant to know who the owners are. They prefer to have the tenants think they are dealing with a management company. This way there is an organized management program and the tenants have to fit into it. Everyone gets treated the same way. This makes everything nice and impersonal and takes a lot of pressure off the landlord, who can say, "It's not my decision. I just work for the management company."

The Phantom Management Company

One small investor we know uses this approach. He owns only four or five properties, but he doesn't want his tenants to know this. He's afraid that they will try to take advantage of him and push him around. Therefore, he created his own company.

He didn't go to the state department of corporations and file all the necessary papers. He didn't even go to the city hall to get a business license. All he did was get a second phone line put into his house and hook it up to an automatic answering service. This is the phone line he uses in all his rental ads and the number he gives to all his tenants.

When people call this number, someone with an aristocratic-sounding English accent (not the property owner) informs them that they have reached the offices of Northside Realty and asks them to leave a message.

Other landlords we know have all their forms and rental contracts printed up using the name of a nonexistent management company for the same reason. (We don't have to do this because, with over one hundred single-family houses, we do have our own management company.)

The Millionaire Landlord

Other landlords use a more direct approach. They let the tenants know who is the owner, and they leave no doubt about what type of landlord they are. One very successful landlord we know tells his tenants that he is a millionaire right off the bat.

"Have you ever dealt with a millionaire?" he asks them. "Well, let me tell you. As long as you do what you're supposed to do, we'll get along fine. But if you ever cross me, you will be sorry, because I have the time and the money to make you regret it. I don't have to work. I don't have any job that I have to go to every day, so I can spend as much time and as much money as I need to if I have to hire every lawyer in this city or this whole state just to get even. So if you're even thinking about causing me any trouble, you'd better leave now."

The Poor Landlord

Other successful landlords take the opposite approach: They play at being poor. When they visit their properties, they wear old clothes and drive an old car. Their idea is to plead poverty. That way, when they have a tenant problem, they can throw it right back at the tenant. For example, when a tenant is late with his rent, "poor" landlords don't make threats. They make the tenant feel guilty. They say something like: "Joe, what are we going to do? We've got a problem here. If you don't pay your rent, I can't make the payment, and we're both going to lose the house. That's no good for either one of us. How are we going to work this out?"

The tenant is stumped. Since all his sob stories and excuses are designed to deal with threats and ultimatums, they are pointless. This approach is something he didn't expect, so he doesn't know how to deal with it. Suddenly, you are on his side and he has to deal with the problem. Since the problem is him, this leaves him confused and defensive. Ideally, he will pay his rent to avoid losing the house. Or he may move out right away because he believes that you're going to lose the house and he'll have to get out anyway.

HOUSES AND SMALL APARTMENT BUILDINGS

Whichever technique you use, make the tenant feel as though he is part of the process. You have to make your tenants feel that they have a future in the house and that it's in their best interest to protect that future by obeying all the rules you lay down and by taking care of your house.

This is why we keep saying "house" instead of "apartment" or "unit." We buy only houses and small income units. People don't feel as though they have any future in an apartment complex. True, you can get more income from large apartment buildings; it's easier to get positive cash flow that way. But you don't get the kinds of tenants we want, or the kinds of tenants that we like to manage.

We want good, responsible, hardworking middle Americans; the kind of people who work with their hands, not with their minds. We want people who do real work—people who do things, create things, and fix things. These are the people who made America and the ones who keep it going. These people make the best tenants. They believe in the work ethic, take pride in their homes, and are not afraid to do minor repairs themselves.

People like this don't want to live in apartments. They want to put down roots, and they see renting a house as the first step toward owning one. They can raise a family in a rental house. They can spread out and feel at home. They can't do that in an apartment.

The type of people we rent to want and need garages. They park and repair their cars in there, and they also may need the garage for storage. They have bats, bikes, and garden tools to store. They wouldn't have any place to keep all of this in an apartment.

If they are family oriented, they also like a backyard for pets and children. They like to have barbecues and family picnics. They want a place for their children to play. They want a place to keep their dogs. They want to keep the house nice, so the dogs stay in the yard. Needless to say, this is fine with us.

But most of all, our kind of tenants want privacy. In an apartment, tenants can feel the neighbors breathing down their necks and hear them walking upstairs. They have to keep the television volume down and be careful when they yell at the kids. An apartment, no matter how nice it may be, just doesn't feel like home. Our tenants may rent an apartment if they have to, but they won't be satisfied with that. They will move to a house as soon as they can.

We provide them with something they can be satisfied with, something they can feel good about. Their hope is always to move up and own a home of their own, and renting a house is the next best alternative for them. Many people will never realize their dreams of home ownership with today's prices and interest rates. Therefore, they need an acceptable substitute.

Renting one of our homes gives them most of the benefits of home ownership without the financial burdens. We do all we can to encourage them to think of it as their own home, and some of them stay with us for years. This is good for them, and more importantly, it is good for us. It makes our program run smoothly, with a minimum of friction and turnover.

STABILITY IS GOLDEN

The less time we have to spend on finding new tenants and breaking them in, the happier we are. This leaves us free to concentrate on other things. It also puts more money in our pockets, since long-term, stable tenants not only mean an uninterrupted stream of rental income, but they also take better care of the property and make fewer demands on us.

When tenants move out, things always have to be done. Paint needs to be freshened, shrubbery needs to be trimmed, and everything has to be spruced up to appeal to the new renters.

Once people are settled into a house, they take care of those things themselves. They have pictures on the walls, and other things in the rooms to distract them. They don't notice that the paint is no longer sparkling fresh. If they do, they can repaint. It is *their* home. They are committed to living there and making it livable, but prospective tenants don't have that commitment yet. They expect things to be more nearly perfect when they move in, and it takes time and effort to get a house into that move-in condition.

PETS AND CHILDREN WELCOME

This is why our whole program is geared toward finding stable tenants. This is why we ignore the conventional wisdom about never renting to people who have pets and children. We want them, or rather, we want the kind of adults that pets and children live with.

Generally speaking, single people are neither stable nor long-term tenants. Sure, there are exceptions to this rule, but for the most part single people's lives are in flux. They have nothing tying them down. They can pick up and go tomorrow if job opportunities, romance, or whim dictates a sudden move.

Another point to consider is that singles are not normally the world's best housekeepers. They have no reason to be. They aren't home-oriented. For them, life is outside the house, where they can meet other singles. When they are home, they usually like to party. Again, there are exceptions to the rule, but for the most part, frequent partying means wear and tear on the house. Drinks get spilled, cigarettes burn the carpet, and walls get scratched and marred.

With single tenants, you can never be quite sure who is living in your house. Roommates, boyfriends, girlfriends, and temporary guests come and go, and none of them feels any responsibility for your house. They are too busy living their lives to bother with maintenance and repairs themselves, so either you do it or it doesn't get done.

Families have a different orientation. They have kids in the local schools and they make friends with the neighbors. The house and the neighborhood become the central focus of their lives. They have more of themselves invested in the house. It is important to them. It's much more than just a temporary crash pad.

This is why we buy three-bedroom, two-bathroom houses—they're family houses. There are plenty of two-bedroom houses and three-bedroom, one-bathroom houses; many of them might be good deals, but they don't fit into our rental program.

Our program is completely geared to buying rental houses that will attract good tenants. We also sometimes buy houses that don't fit into the program, but we don't hold onto them. If they're really good deals, with a lot of free equity to be picked up, we buy them for immediate resale and a quick profit. Let owner occupants buy them, or someone else buy them as rentals. We don't need them.

PREVENTING PEOPLE PROBLEMS

Since people cause 99 percent of the problems associated with owning rental property, then common sense says that you can eliminate those problems by eliminating the wrong kinds of tenants. For example, who is going to destroy your property? Are good tenants going to cause damage? No, not unless they have a bad landlord who has been mistreating them and they want to get even.

Or, unless they don't know how to avoid damaging the property because they are ignorant. There are people who simply don't know how to take care of a house, particularly if they have never lived in one before. If they have spent their lives in apartments, where the landlord or the building superintendent took care of everything, they may not know how to do anything for themselves.

This does not necessarily make them bad people, or bad tenants. They just have to be educated. Some single-family homeowners who rent out dozens of houses hold seminars for their tenants, showing them how to maintain a house and do simple repairs. If the tenants don't want to attend, they don't rent the house. It's as simple as that.

Another man we know manages over 450 single-family houses (about three hundred of them are his own). He produced a little pamphlet telling people how to be good tenants. The booklet starts with his rules and regulations, all the dos and don'ts he has developed after twenty years of owning rental houses. It then goes into helpful household hints: how to keep houses clean, dry, and well maintained. The pamphlet tells how to recognize bugs, how to avoid them, and how to get rid of them once they appear. It also includes tips on weatherproofing and sealing windows and doors to conserve heat and save money.

It pays to invest time in your tenants by doing things like this. You should learn to look at landlord-tenant relations like bank savings. The more you put in, the more you will get back. It's as simple as that. Treat your tenants as though they are an integral and important part of your management team. After all, you are counting on them to work with you to keep things running smoothly and to keep the money rolling in.

You wouldn't turn an employee loose with an expensive piece of machinery and no instructions to operate it. Why should you do this with your tenants? No matter how good they are, no matter how loyal they are and eager to please, they can't live up to your expectations until they know and understand what those expectations are. Don't be afraid to set high standards for your tenants. If you pick the right people to begin with, and treat them with courtesy and respect, they will usually try to live up to this treatment. When they do, you should reward them.

REWARDS AND INCENTIVES FOR GOOD TENANTS

It's important to set up a system of rewards and incentives for your tenants just like those that some companies offer their best employees. You can discount their rent if it's paid on time. You can offer them paint or some other amenities to help improve the house.

You can even help them celebrate their anniversary. When they have been with you for a year, do something for them. Let them know that you care. Let them know you appreciate them as good tenants. Encourage them to stay another year, and another one, and another one. Give them the free use of a handyman for the day, or at least part of the day. Give them a special one-time rent rebate of $25 or $50. (This can even work out to be cheaper than the handyman-for-the-day idea, and it can build a lot of goodwill.)

Gestures like this pay off. Tenants do appreciate them, and they'll tell their friends. This is how one good tenant leads to another. Wouldn't it be nice to fill all your vacancies with people who have been referred to you by current and previous good tenants? This way you know whom you're getting, and they know what to expect from you.

Proper tenant management can eliminate almost all your rental nightmares. Late rent? No rent at all? The problem comes from you as much from your tenants. You must be doing something to give them the idea they can get away with this. If you aren't serious about having the rent paid on time, why should they be?

Ask yourself if you set up clear guidelines right from the beginning. Did you make it clear that the rent was due on a certain day and that there were no exceptions? Did you make any effort to be flexible, to work with them to set up a mutually agreeable day for them to pay the rent?

Not everyone is comfortable paying his rent on the first of the month. What if he gets paid on the fifth? Or the fifteenth? Whenever possible, you should set a date that the tenant feels good about. Be flexible, but once the date is set, do not tolerate excuses. If he agrees to pay the rent by the tenth of each month, the eleventh or the twelfth won't do. Make sure that all your tenants understand this right from the beginning, and you shouldn't have any problems later. Let them know that they will be treated fairly as long as they obey the rules, and that they will be thrown out promptly if they break them.

Punishment for Bad Tenants

No one likes evictions. Going to court is ugly: it is nasty, expensive, and time-consuming. Unfortunately, even the best landlord makes the occasional mistake, and the only way to deal with it is to move promptly. There is absolutely no excuse for a tenant to stay on if he is not paying the rent. As soon as the payment is late, the residents of the house should receive a formal notice informing them of the consequences. Let them know that they will be evicted as soon as the law allows. There will not be a month or two of sob stories or excuses about why they can't pay now.

You are a landlord, not a moneylender. If the tenants can't pay the rent, let them borrow the money, or go on welfare. You can't afford to treat them as charity cases. If your primary interest is to help people solve all their problems, then you will be more effective as a social worker than as a landlord.

Being a landlord means that you have to be tough, especially in the beginning. You can't be overly friendly with your tenants; you have to remain cool and businesslike. You can loosen up later, once the tenants have proven themselves, but not in the beginning. If you're looking for new friends, join a hobby club, don't buy rental property.

On the other hand, you can't be too hard-nosed either. After all, tenants are people, too. If you choose them right and treat them fairly, they'll work with you. If you mistreat and abuse them, sooner or later they will rebel.

Rebellious Tenants

Tenant rebellions can take any of several forms, and none of them is particularly pleasant for the landlord. The least costly form, and the one that takes the least time and effort to solve, is that your tenants simply move out. This usually means that you must repaint and clean the house, then advertise and show the property to prospective new tenants, and check out the best applicants.

The next level of tenant rebellion is neglecting your property. This includes letting the lawn and plants die while weeds sprout up everywhere, leaving trash around the yard or even inside the house, letting the kids draw on the walls, allowing the carpets to become soiled, and letting minor maintenance jobs go until they become major problems. The tenants rationalize this by thinking: "The landlord doesn't care about us, so why should we worry about him and his house?" And if you've treated them unfairly, you really have only yourself to blame for this attitude.

When the property reaches the point where it's practically unsuitable for human habitation, if you're lucky these tenants will simply move, leaving you with a huge—and often expensive—job replacing the landscaping and getting the house back into decent shape. If you're not so lucky, these tenants will simply let everything slide further and further downhill until you're forced to evict them. Then you have all the expenses in time and money of going through the courts before you're left with an empty, filthy property to work on.

The third outlet for rebellious tenants is deliberate vandalism. Sure, it's against the law for anyone to tear out fixtures, break windows, remove paneling, and maybe even set fire to someone else's property. But you have to catch the culprits and prove they did it before the law can punish them. Tenants who go this far usually know that. Most of them will do their dark deeds in the middle of the night, right after they pack up everything they own and just before they take off for the other end of the country, leaving no forwarding address.

Of course, landlords do sometimes catch up with vandalizing tenants. Then it's possible to get a judgment requiring them to pay for what they did. If the damage is bad enough, the tenants may even go to jail for a while. But collecting on the judgment is the landlord's job, and often an impossible one. Besides, getting a judgment or throwing the tenant in jail may satisfy your thirst for revenge, but it won't fix up your property. That job will still be waiting for you when you're through playing cops and robbers and talking to the judge.

The fourth kind of tenant rebellion is organizing or joining a rent-control movement. This is one of the most serious problems that can arise between landlords and tenants. The results are long-lasting, because once in place, rent control can be with you much longer than any particular tenant or group of tenants. Rent control can even drive you out of the landlording business, and it will discourage others from entering it.

This means, naturally, that eventually there won't be any decent rental housing in rent-controlled areas. Why, then, would tenants want to get involved in something that will lead to renters being unable to find well-maintained, desirable housing?

What Kinds of Tenants Push for Rent Control?

Ask yourself what type of tenant votes for rent control. Think about it for a minute. Rent control sounds like a great idea. The only problem is that it doesn't work. Experience has shown this again and again, in place after place. It doesn't benefit tenants, it hurts them. Maintenance goes down, the area goes to pot, and everyone is unhappy. Therefore, there are only three main types of tenants who would vote for rent control.

Professional Radicals.   The first group is made up of professional radicals and agitators. These are the people who know damned well that rent control doesn't work, but they don't care. For them it is an instrument of social change, the first shot in the class war they want to start between the haves and the have-nots.

There is only one way to deal with these people: avoid them like the plague. They are bad news, and they are not the ones you want to rent to. They will gripe and complain about everything and have you in court at the drop of a hat. They will also try to organize your other tenants and get them to stir up trouble, too.

Ignorant Victims.   The second group is just plain ignorant and/or not very bright. They believe what they hear, and they hear that rent control will lower their rents. You have to deal with these people the way you deal with children. You have to patiently teach them and explain to them what rent control really does.

Tell them right out that rent control means less money for you and less service for them. How can you stay on top of maintenance when you have less rent money coming in? You might even have to sell the house if it becomes unprofitable to hold it as a rental, and then they would have to move. Is that really going to benefit them?

Abused Tenants.   The last group is composed of tenants who feel, rightly or wrongly, that they have been abused. They don't like you, and rent control is their way of getting even. By the time it gets to that point, it is too late to deal with them effectively. You have already made your mistakes. Either you never should have rented to them in the first place, or you should have made them feel better about renting from you. It is just like any other business. If management and labor are getting along and everyone is happy, then who needs unions? They come into the picture only when there are friction and disputes.

If you are a good landlord, a good people manager, you will not have to worry about tenants' unions or rent control. You won't have to worry about late rents and costly evictions. These things will happen occasionally, but not often enough to be a serious problem.

Now that you know what types of tenants to look for and how to manage them, the next step is finding the right properties to attract them.

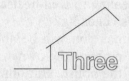

Three

Buy Right to Manage Right

Many people make the mistake of buying "bargain" properties only to discover that they don't make good rentals. They buy a property because it is priced $10,000 or $20,000 below the fair-market value—or so they are told—but the rental income won't cover the payments. They have to take money out of their pockets each month just to support their great deal. But of course they assume they will get back all they've put into the property and more, if they can just hang on and wait for the property to appreciate.

BEWARE OF DISCOUNT PRICING

Does this sound familiar? Have you ever been caught by this approach to real estate investing? A lot of people have. It's a common mistake for inexperienced investors to make. Greed overrides common sense. All people see is the "discount" they are getting on the price.

There are several major problems with that approach. The main one is that the discount is worthless until the house is actually sold. Until then, you are stuck with a negative cash flow. This makes the house a good candidate for quick turnover if you can find someone to pay you more for it than you did.

A home owner with a good income would be your best prospect. However, you have to ask yourself a question: If the house is so appealing to well-heeled home buyers, why were you able to buy it so cheaply?

Sometimes you will be able to come up with a reason. For example, perhaps the owner was in financial trouble and had to get rid of the house. But other times, you won't have any clear proof that the house is really worth more than you paid for it. This is when you realize that you really made a mistake. The payments may be so high that no one wants the house—not even home buyers. That's when you're in trouble; you have a gorilla on your back. What do you do then? You don't want it and you can't get rid of it. The only way to avoid this when you buy property is to think about more than the price. Think about the realistic resale value when you're buying for quick turnover. If you really think you can get rid of the property in a short period of time, then the negative cash flow isn't important. It just becomes another business expense you deduct from the profits, and you still come out way ahead.

If you're buying a house for a rental, the price is relatively unimportant. What is more important are the terms. If you're wealthy and you can afford a negative cash flow, that's one thing; maybe you can even use the tax write-off. But if you can't, you have no business buying property with negative cash flow for a rental, even if you get the house for $100,000 or $200,000 under the market value. You will have to ask top-dollar rents in order to minimize your losses. You're going to rush to get a tenant in there, and you won't be careful enough. If the property is such a great buy, then turn it over for a quick profit, but don't keep it for a rental.

There is another, even more basic mistake you might make if you get too wrapped up in the price. The house may not even be a good rental property, aside from the negative cash flow. It may not be the type of place that good tenants will be attracted to.

FINDING GOOD RENTALS

To get good tenants, you must buy properties in a good area. That's the first rule. The type of tenants you want to attract don't rent houses. They rent schools, transportation, shopping, and churches. They rent where the jobs are or where the jobs will be, especially in these hard times. Do you take these things into consideration when you buy rental property? You'd better. Is the area going up or down? Is industry moving in or out? Are jobs being created or lost? What is the forecast for the future? Who will you rent to, and how much will they be able to pay? What kinds of jobs will they work at, and how much will their salaries be?

The real profits in rental property come when you get steady increases in rental income and market value. Each year your income and your net worth go up. This is the way it's supposed to work, but it happens only when you buy in the right areas. If you buy property in areas that are dying, you will get some great buys, but what will you do with them? There will be almost no one to rent to, and those who do want to rent from you may not have money or jobs. How much rent can they pay? What are the chances that you will get your rent each month?

How can you run a business unless you are reasonably sure that your customers will pay their bills? If you have no steady source of income, you have no business. Yet many people jump into rental properties with no idea of how to rent them out. They are trying to run a service business, but they have no idea what sort of service their customers, their prospective tenants, want. These investors are buying property for all the wrong reasons and not even taking the right ones into account.

We always look at the properties we buy as rental properties, through a tenant's eyes. If the property won't appeal to tenants, more specifically to our kinds of tenants, we won't buy it unless we are sure we can turn it over for a quick profit.

Why should we create problems for ourselves? There are enough things that can go wrong when you are a landlord, so why compound your problems by being lazy? There's a lot of money to be made in real estate, but it isn't free money. You do have to work for it. Part of that work is doing your homework first, so you can save yourself a lot of grief later.

WHAT ARE TENANTS LOOKING FOR?

If you read the previous chapter, you know what type of tenant you are looking for. Now put yourself in their place. Where would you want to live? Why? Would you want to live in the property you are thinking of buying? What does the property have to offer: Is it attractive? *Could* it be attractive? What are the neighboring properties like? Who lives in the neighborhood? What do they do for a living? Do they do anything for a living?

People tend to congregate with their own kind. If you buy in a good neighborhood, you should attract good tenants. If you buy in a trashy area, you are likely to attract trash for tenants. Ask yourself: Who will the tenants' children play with? Juvenile delinquents? Or honor students?

If you want working people, middle-class Americans, you buy houses in middle-class, blue-collar neighborhoods. You don't buy houses in the wealthier parts of town, and you don't buy them in the slums. You don't buy houses in student areas unless you want to rent to students. And you don't buy houses any-where near a college or university unless you want to rent to students, professors, administrators, and other well-educated white-collar tenants.

Do students make great tenants? Well, if you own cheap apartments, you can jam in a lot of young people at outrageous rents. Of course, you have to deal with constant turnover and vandalism, not to mention plain old negligence. Think back to what it was like when you were in college. Now ask yourself if you would want to rent to someone like that.

How about professors and other college employees? They are used to delaying all their other bills, so why should they pay you on time? They are sophisticated. They know how to play games with money and people. They also know their rights. They know all you are supposed to do for them, and more, and they aren't afraid to call you in the middle of the night to complain if some-thing is wrong.

You want to stay away from wealthy areas for the same rea-son. Whom will you be renting to if you buy a fancy house that rents for $1,500 a month? Assuming you can actually get that

kind of rent, you will be dealing with high rollers, slick opera-
tors, and very demanding types. Not exactly the salt of the
earth.

The guy who comes to fix the plumbing or the television set
doesn't expect to go home to a mansion at night, just something
comfortable. Charlie Coveralls, the guy who works down at the
factory or up at the construction site, can't afford $1,500 a
month. About $450 or $500 is probably all he can handle, and
maybe a lot less than that.

Take this into consideration when you look at an area. If it
looks too wealthy, it's no good. Joggers are a telltale sign, because they tend to be professional people and white-collar workers. It might be a great area for speculation, since more
expensive houses tend to appreciate faster, but it is not a good
rental area.

On the other hand, you don't want to buy in an area where
most of the houses are rentals. You want to buy in an area that
is mostly owner-occupied. No one given a choice wants to live
in a rental area. Areas with a heavy rate of owner occupancy
are usually nicer and better kept, since home owners take better
care of their houses than most landlords or tenants do.

If you buy houses in areas that are primarily owner occupied,
you will help your tenants keep their dream alive. If they're
surrounded by home owners, they'll keep dreaming of owning
their own home. They'll treat your home as if it is theirs, and
they'll take better care of it.

Of course, this works only if the rest of the houses in the
neighborhood are well kept. Unfortunately, home owners can
be lazy and slovenly, too, especially in declining neighborhoods.
Some of them neglect their properties just the way many landlords do. If this is what your tenants see around them, this is
what they're likely to emulate.

The neighbors are very important when you buy rental property. They can help make or break your rental business. Good
neighbors are a pleasure to live near, and many times tenants
are reluctant to pack up and move once they've established ties
with their neighbors.

The neighbors can also help you keep your tenants in line. If
your tenants know that you're friendly with the neighbors and

that the neighbors will keep·you informed, it can make a big difference. Some tenants need to know that "Big Brother" is always watching them.

And, of course, good neighbors help prevent crime by looking out for each other and scaring away burglars. This can be an important selling point when you rent a house. Everybody wants to live in a low-crime area.

CHECKING OUT THE NEIGHBORHOOD

Drive around the area. Park for a while and think about what you see. Does the area look neat, attractive, and appealing? What about the individual houses? What do you think about the people you see on the streets?

Look at the cars. What kind are they, and what condition are they in? Do they look well kept? The way people keep their cars often tells you a lot about the way they keep their houses. Cars also tell you a lot about the owners' life-styles. Think about it for a minute, and you'll realize that the rich and the poor often drive the same kinds of cars. Therefore, you want to stay away from areas where you see too many new Cadillacs (although our kind of people often drive older Cadillacs in mint or near-mint condition). You want to see pickup trucks and American cars, but not jacked up and parked on the front lawn. If you don't see what you want, or you don't like what you see, move on, no matter how sweet a deal the house seems to be.

Look for well-kept residential areas, modest but proud areas where tenants will feel happy and privileged to live in your house. Ride around on Sundays and find neighborhoods where people are out mowing their lawns and polishing their cars. After all, isn't that the spirit you want your tenants to have?

Find out where the stores, the schools, the parks, and entertainment facilities are located. See how far away they are and how convenient they are to get to. Can you walk to the store? to the schools? Can tenants get around on public transportation? Are there freeways nearby? What does the neighborhood have to recommend it?

You want to buy properties that are near shopping and transportation, but not next door to them. Living on a busy commercial street or in a heavy industrial area next to factories and warehouses is rarely anyone's idea of paradise. Buying houses like that will not assure you of getting long-term, stable tenants.

LOOKING AT THE HOUSE

You need to know about the neighborhood before you even begin to worry about the property itself, but the property is important. When all is said and done, prospective tenants will make their decision based on whether or not they like the house.

What features do you look for in a house? What features do tenants expect? We've already talked about a backyard and a garage, but what type of backyard? What type of garage? This can be important.

If the other houses in the neighborhood have big yards and your yard is small, that could make the house less desirable. People want good-sized yards when they have families and pets. They want yards that are usable, not merely decorative. Only singles and other people who are away from home a lot want "low-maintenance" postage-stamp-sized yards. The same thing goes for garages. If most of the houses in the area have double garages, and yours is a small single garage, you could be out of the market.

These are facts of life. You can ignore them, but that won't make them go away. If you want to be a successful landlord, you have to know about these things. You have to take them into consideration whenever you look at a house, and the yard and garage are only the beginning.

Inside, what is the kitchen like? Is it modern? Is there a garbage disposal and a dishwasher? Women buy houses, and they also rent them. If the husband likes it but the wife doesn't, eight couples out of ten will pass the house up. However, if the wife likes it and the husband doesn't, at least six out of ten will take it anyway. Women are often the ones who spend more time at home, and they are usually the ones who care about the kitchen and what it looks like. Try to make the kitchen look light and airy. Make sure it's clean. If the kitchen doesn't look attractive, most good tenants will be scared off. These people will have no trouble finding another place—with a clean, attractive kitchen —to rent. You will be stuck with the bad tenants, the ones who can't rent anything better because nobody wants them.

Bathrooms are important, too. If there's only one bathroom, you can expect less rent than you could get for a house with two bathrooms. Besides that, if the bathrooms are filthy and unattractive when the average woman looks at the house, all she will see is work—hard, ugly work. Would you want to get down on your knees to scrub someone else's dirt off the bathroom floor?

All the windows in the house should be washed. That way the house will be light and cheery. A light house shows better because it looks bigger and more comfortable than a dark, closed-in house. Plants grow better in light houses, too, which adds to their attractiveness.

The floors should also be clean. This is something else that women notice. Clean carpets, linoleum, and wood floors make a big difference. They set the tone for the house and make it look inviting. Dirty floors make it look shabby and run-down.

Bedrooms are easy to deal with. All they have are windows and bare walls, so a little bit of fresh paint goes a long way. It's not hard to make them attractive, but make sure that the house needs only cosmetic work.

In fact, that holds true for the entire house. You don't want to find out that the minor cracks you plastered and painted over will keep reappearing almost as fast as you cover them up. This would indicate that you might have a serious, or at the least a very annoying problem with the house. The way you avoid surprises like this is to get an inspection before you buy the property. You put into the contract that the deal is contingent upon your approval of a structural inspection report, and then you hire someone to go over the property thoroughly and tell you what is wrong with it.

KNOW WHAT YOU'RE BUYING

Almost any property is going to have some problems, and you want to know what they are, and, ideally, have the seller correct them before you close escrow. Even if the seller refuses, you still want to know what the problems are so that you can correct them yourself.

You can hire a licensed contractor or a handyman to make these inspections, but be careful. If the person you hire thinks that he is also going to do the repair work, he may look for things to do. He may also inflate prices, if he thinks he can get away with it. There are many fine, upstanding, honest, and hard-working contractors out there, but there are also a lot of crooks and swindlers.

Therefore, it's usually best to try to find an inspection service that does nothing but inspections. You can find them in the phone book under "building inspections" and "contractors" or "structural engineers." Many inspection services are run by retired contractors who got tired of doing the work and decided that doing inspections is easier. Since they don't bid on jobs, they have no reason to give you anything but honest quotes. They'll usually tell you what's worth fixing and what isn't, since they aren't trying to make work for themselves.

Of course, if you have a good handyman that you trust, you can use him to do your inspections. It depends on you and whatever you're comfortable with. But remember, the more thorough you are before you buy, the fewer problems you're likely to have later.

We get the most thorough inspection possible on every house we buy because we do everything we can to cut down on maintenance problems. We try to buy houses that are no more than ten years old. We look for well-built tract homes that aren't starting to come apart yet and that won't deteriorate for at least another ten years, since we intend to hold them for five years. Houses like these have their problems, but they're usually minor. Carpeting and linoleum wear out and need to be replaced, but all the vital systems—electrical, plumbing, and structural—are in excellent shape. We don't buy junk, because we don't want to manage it. We don't want to own anything that's suffering from deferred maintenance. There are too many good houses out there for us to waste our time on the poor ones.

Have your inspector check the foundation. If the house isn't on a solid foundation, you could lose it someday. It could shift and be severely damaged, or even destroyed. Look for cracks and leaks where water may be coming in and for any other signs of potential trouble.

Then check the wiring, plumbing, and sewer lines. These are the things people can't live without. Bad wiring can burn a house down, and bad plumbing can quickly make it unlivable. If the house needs rewiring or replumbing, you want to know 'this before you commit yourself to buying it.

That kind of information can seriously affect the price and the terms. Those are expensive jobs, and you would want the seller to pay for them in one way or another. You don't pay full price for a house unless you know what you're getting into and that the house is in good condition. Even the littlest things add up— the windows, the gutters, the shrubbery that has to be planted in the yard. If these small items cost you fifty dollars here and fifty dollars there, before you know it, you've got thousands of dollars in unexpected expenses. This is an unprofitable and therefore intolerable situation. You've got to know these details in advance; otherwise you're throwing money away.

Prepare an Inspection Checklist

In order to ensure that you cover everything, you should make up a checklist, like the one on the following pages, of all the major features and systems in the houses you look at. Grade them from "Excellent" to "Needs Repair." This will give you an idea of what you are getting into.

You can then use this same sort of checklist with tenants to let them know what's in good shape when they move in and to make it clear to them that everything had better be in the same condition when they move out. This helps prevent arguments about security deposits and damage claims.

In business terms, this is just basic inventory control. After all, you are in the rental business, so your houses are your inventory. They are your stock in trade, your company's reason to exist. If you don't keep track of them and maintain them in good condition, you won't be in business very long.

PROPERTY EXTERIOR CHECKLIST

Address _____

Tenant's Name _____

Appearance of Grounds (General)
Describe in Detail Condition of Lawn and Plantings
Common Areas, Blacktop, Walks, Driveways, Pool
Lighting and Sprinklers
Garages or Carports
Condition of Roofs
Condition of Exterior Walls in Detail

	OK	NOT	Additional Comments
Garage	[ ]	[ ]	_____
Carport	[ ]	[ ]	_____
Patio	[ ]	[ ]	_____
Storage Room	[ ]	[ ]	_____
Doors			
—Louvers Intact	[ ]	[ ]	_____
—Locks	[ ]	[ ]	_____
—Latches	[ ]	[ ]	_____
—Surfaces	[ ]	[ ]	_____
—Doorstops	[ ]	[ ]	_____
Nameholders	[ ]	[ ]	_____
Doorbell	[ ]	[ ]	_____
Washer			
—Serial #	[ ]	[ ]	_____
—Hookup	[ ]	[ ]	_____
Dryer			
—Serial #	[ ]	[ ]	_____
—Hookup	[ ]	[ ]	_____
Other:			
_____	[ ]	[ ]	_____
_____	[ ]	[ ]	_____

General Remarks:_____
_____

Inspected by: _____   Date: _____
              _____   Date: _____

I (we) have inspected the above facilities and agree they are in good working condition except as noted.

_____   _____
Tenant   Date

_____   _____
Tenant   Date

PROPERTY INTERIOR CHECKLIST

Kitchen	OK	NOT	Additional Comments
Floors clean	[ ]	[ ]	_____
Disposal works	[ ]	[ ]	_____
Sink stopper	[ ]	[ ]	_____
Strainer	[ ]	[ ]	_____
Sink chips	[ ]	[ ]	_____
Countertops	[ ]	[ ]	_____
Range hood clean	[ ]	[ ]	_____
Cabinets	[ ]	[ ]	_____
Exhaust fan works	[ ]	[ ]	_____
Dishwasher	[ ]	[ ]	_____
—Serial #	[ ]	[ ]	_____
Refrigerator	[ ]	[ ]	_____
—Serial #	[ ]	[ ]	_____
—Clean	[ ]	[ ]	_____
—Light OK	[ ]	[ ]	_____
—Trays OK	[ ]	[ ]	_____
—Shelves OK	[ ]	[ ]	_____
Range	[ ]	[ ]	_____
—Serial #	[ ]	[ ]	_____
—Interior clean	[ ]	[ ]	_____
—Knobs OK	[ ]	[ ]	_____
—Pans/racks OK	[ ]	[ ]	_____
Light switches	[ ]	[ ]	_____
Bulbs	[ ]	[ ]	_____
Windows	[ ]	[ ]	_____
Screens	[ ]	[ ]	_____
Door	[ ]	[ ]	_____
Walls	[ ]	[ ]	_____
Overall clean	[ ]	[ ]	_____
Other:			
_____	[ ]	[ ]	_____
_____	[ ]	[ ]	_____
Dining/Living			
Floors	[ ]	[ ]	_____
Carpets	[ ]	[ ]	_____
Lights	[ ]	[ ]	_____
Windows	[ ]	[ ]	_____
Screens	[ ]	[ ]	_____
Walls	[ ]	[ ]	_____
Wood paneling	[ ]	[ ]	_____
Drapes	[ ]	[ ]	_____
Drapery rods	[ ]	[ ]	_____
Other:			
_____	[ ]	[ ]	_____
_____	[ ]	[ ]	_____

PROPERTY INTERIOR CHECKLIST (continued)

Bathroom(s)	OK	NOT	Additional Comments
First	[ ]	[ ]	_____
Toilet OK	[ ]	[ ]	_____
Faucets OK	[ ]	[ ]	_____
Sink chips	[ ]	[ ]	_____
T. Paper roll OK	[ ]	[ ]	_____
Stoppers work	[ ]	[ ]	_____
Mirrors OK	[ ]	[ ]	_____
Bars OK	[ ]	[ ]	_____
Curtain rod	[ ]	[ ]	_____
Fixtures	[ ]	[ ]	_____
Tile	[ ]	[ ]	_____
Tub caulking	[ ]	[ ]	_____
Tub chips	[ ]	[ ]	_____
Bulbs	[ ]	[ ]	_____
Switches	[ ]	[ ]	_____
Vent fan works	[ ]	[ ]	_____
Floors OK	[ ]	[ ]	_____
Window	[ ]	[ ]	_____
Other:			
_____	[ ]	[ ]	_____
_____	[ ]	[ ]	_____
Bedrooms:			
First			
Walls	[ ]	[ ]	_____
Floors	[ ]	[ ]	_____
Carpets	[ ]	[ ]	_____
Lights	[ ]	[ ]	_____
Windows	[ ]	[ ]	_____
Screens	[ ]	[ ]	_____
Closets	[ ]	[ ]	_____
Other:			
_____	[ ]	[ ]	_____
_____	[ ]	[ ]	_____
Second			
Walls	[ ]	[ ]	_____
Floors	[ ]	[ ]	_____
Carpets	[ ]	[ ]	_____
Lights	[ ]	[ ]	_____
Windows	[ ]	[ ]	_____
Screens	[ ]	[ ]	_____
Closets	[ ]	[ ]	_____
Other:			
_____	[ ]	[ ]	_____
_____	[ ]	[ ]	_____

PROPERTY INTERIOR CHECKLIST (continued)

Third	OK	NOT	Additional Comments
Walls	[ ]	[ ]	_____
Floors	[ ]	[ ]	_____
Carpets	[ ]	[ ]	_____
Lights	[ ]	[ ]	_____
Windows	[ ]	[ ]	_____
Screens	[ ]	[ ]	_____
Closets	[ ]	[ ]	_____
Other:			
_____	[ ]	[ ]	_____
_____	[ ]	[ ]	_____

Fourth	OK	NOT	Additional Comments
Walls	[ ]	[ ]	_____
Floors	[ ]	[ ]	_____
Carpets	[ ]	[ ]	_____
Lights	[ ]	[ ]	_____
Windows	[ ]	[ ]	_____
Screens	[ ]	[ ]	_____
Closets	[ ]	[ ]	_____
Other:			
_____	[ ]	[ ]	_____
_____	[ ]	[ ]	_____

DATA SHEET

Address _____

Subdivision _____

Purchase Price

$_____

Market Value

$_____

Area

_____

Comps.

1._____

$_____

2._____

$_____

3._____

$_____

	Payment	**Type**	**Due**
1st Loan $____ ____	$_____	_____	_____
2nd Loan $____ ____	$_____	_____	_____
3rd Loan $____ ____	$_____	_____	_____

$____ Plus Costs (closing, paint, drapes, etc.)

Description   **Other**

Age_____   Cool_____   Roof_____   Range_____   1._____

Bdrms _____   Heat _____   Fenced_____   Disp _____   2._____

Baths _____   Firpl _____   Floors_____   Carport _____   3._____

Swft _____   Const _____   Ldscp_____   Refrig _____   4._____

Condition: _____

_____

_____

_____

A checklist can also become a good negotiating tool. How can the seller argue that his property is in excellent shape when you present him with a detailed list of the faults?

Each item on the list is worth money to you. Each fault means one more concession the seller has to make in order to compensate. You might get the price lowered, or get better terms. But whatever it is, you should get something.

Of course, some of you are probably worried that this could backfire. The seller might get insulted by the way you're picking his house apart. He might become less flexible about the price and terms, because his pride is involved. In fact, he might even refuse to sell to you at all.

That's okay, too, so relax and stop worrying. If the seller is that concerned about his pride, then he isn't the seller you want to deal with anyway. You'll never get his house for the best price and terms, so why waste your time with him?

NEGOTIATING WITH SELLERS

Ideally, the sellers you want to deal with don't have any pride left. They've realized that pride is too expensive. They're in trouble and they need to sell quickly; that's their main motivation. They don't have time to be insulted; they need to get rid of the house. Those are the people who will give you the type of deal you want, the kind you need to run a successful rental business.

In today's world, with sky-high prices and interest rates, you have to structure your deal right or you'll get swamped under by negative cash flow. Your income will not nearly cover your expenses, and you will be in big trouble, even before the maintenance problems start.

This is another way that many beginning investors go wrong. They agree to take on a negative cash flow that they can handle, but just barely. Then the first time a maintenance problem occurs, or the roof or the furnace or the refrigerator needs to be replaced, they're in big trouble.

The smart investor-landlord won't put himself into this position. If he can't structure the financing to make the transaction work, he'll walk away from it. No deal is too good to pass up if it won't work comfortably for you. It may be a great deal for someone else who has more money, imagination, or nerve than you do, but that doesn't make it right for you.

So never be afraid to say no! Remember, you have to say yes to the deal before the seller does, and you never have to agree to buy something that's wrong for you. There will be plenty of other properties around, if you just look a little harder. Many people forget this. They become fixated on a particular deal, and they think the seller has the final say on whether or not they can put together a deal.

This isn't a good way to buy property. There's been a lot of talk in the past couple of years about "don't wanter" sellers. These are the people we look for, the ones who don't want their houses or just can't afford to keep them. These are the people who will give you good deals, but only if you know how to handle them and negotiate to get what you want. You have to let them think that they want to sell more than you want to buy. We try to be "don't wanter" buyers. This puts all the burden of salesmanship on the seller.

If we're anxious to buy a property, we might pay too much or make other concessions that we shouldn't. Once you want something, you become emotionally involved, and that's bad business. When we don't want a house, we make a better offer —better for us, that is. It's a take-it-or-leave-it offer based strictly on the numbers. If it's accepted, and we get the house at the price and terms we want, then it will be a good one to add to our portfolio. It will fit right into our program. If we don't get it, we know there are plenty of other houses out there.

Once the seller realizes that this is our attitude, it forces him to think about how badly he wants and needs to sell. He sees that we don't buy houses, we buy terms. If he can and will offer us the right terms, he's got a sale. If he can't or won't offer terms we like, then he's lost us. After all, we're not looking for a home to live in, just a property to use as a rental, an income-producing vehicle. As long as the numbers work and it fits our program, one house is as good as the next one. Sentiment doesn't enter into it.

This keeps us from getting in over our heads. If the seller has to convince us to buy a house we really don't want, then he has to offer us something special. He's on the defensive. He's competing with all the other people who have houses we could buy, and we make sure that he knows this.

We always tell sellers that we are considering at least two or three other houses. This puts the pressure on and gets that old competitive instinct going. If he doesn't get us to buy this house, he has failed. He has been beaten in open competition with other sellers.

The Terms We Want

What does a seller have to do to get us to buy his house? To begin with, he has to have a low-interest, low-balance assumable FHA (Federal Housing Administration) or VA (Veteran's Administration) loan. Why FHA/VA loans? Because they are completely legally assumable. There is no due-on-sale clause written into the original contract. Therefore, they are not affected by all the recent court decisions on the due-on-sale clause.

These old loans make our houses affordable. Low-interest loans mean low monthly payments. Why should we go out and get new loans at 12 percent to 14 percent interest, or even 11 percent when the rates occasionally come down a little? This doesn't make any sense when there are lots of old 8 percent, 9 percent, and 10 percent loans available. You don't make money by giving it away, and you can't run a successful rental business unless you can cut your negative cash flow to a minimum.

This means that sellers who want to deal with us have to be flexible. They have to help us structure affordable payments, payments that we can live with, or the deal won't work. We're not going to burden ourselves with a debt load that the house won't support.

We'll put up with a small bit of negative cash flow, since we usually don't put up any cash down payment, but we have strict limits. If the negative cash flow is going to be more than $75 to $100 a month, the house isn't for us. If we put up down-payment money, there had better be a positive cash flow. This means the seller has to make sacrifices. He can get some cash, if that's what he wants and needs—as long as it doesn't come out of our pockets. However, he won't get all his money up front. And he won't get any monthly payments on the amount he carries back.

If this arrangement won't work for the seller, he had better find someone else to buy his property, because it's usually the only way that will work for us. If we can come to a meeting of the minds, fine. If not, then we find another house. We can afford to be flexible up to a point, but we do have certain definite criteria that we insist upon. We know what works for us. If our way doesn't work for the seller, then there is really no way for us to do business.

We hold to this rule inflexibly. If we started making exceptions, we'd get into trouble. In a way, we treat sellers like tenants. We let them know that we have an organized program that treats everyone the same. They either want to be part of that program, or they don't. If they do, then they have to conform. They have to play by our rules or there's no game.

Not every seller will go along with this. Not every tenant will, either. This is why we don't buy every house we make offers on or rent to every tenant we interview. It's a selection process; some people meet our standards and others don't. Those who meet those standards, who will put themselves out to meet them, are the only ones we deal with.

The One-Two-Three Punch

Our typical deal works on a principle we call the one-two-three punch. We assume the first mortgage, we (or the seller) get a second mortgage that supplies the seller with cash for his down payment, and the seller carries a third mortgage for the balance.

This is how we get into houses with little or no money down and still keep the payments affordable. For example, let's say we buy a house for $55,000. It has a $25,000 FHA loan at 8 percent interest with payments of $183 a month. But that leaves a gap of $30,000. Where is that money going to come from?

We don't have $30,000 cash that we want to put into the deal, so we ask the seller to carry that amount as a third mortgage. The seller doesn't want to carry paper. He wants his $30,000 in cash. We explain to him that we don't buy property that way, and we compromise. We give him $10,000 in cash generated through a 15-year amortized second mortgage against the property.

At 14 percent interest, this will add another $171 a month to the payment. That means the payments on the first and the second total $354 a month. The taxes and insurance bring it up to close to $500 a month. The house will rent for only $350, so we can't really afford to pay any more on top of that. Therefore, the seller has to carry the remaining $20,000 of his equity without any monthly payments.

Balloon Payments

This leads to the inevitable: a balloon payment. There's no getting around it, but we make sure that we put it off for at least five to seven years. By then we will have enough equity in the house so that we can sell it or refinance it. In the meantime, the payments are affordable and the negative cash flow is kept to a minimum.

Whenever possible, we don't pay any interest on the third. We offer the seller full price for his house, but he has to accept our terms. Some sellers eat this up. Others refuse to carry paper without getting at least some interest. In that case, we usually have to lower the price.

Not every seller will go along with this arrangement, but we deal only with the ones who will. We meet a lot of initial resistance to the idea of a five-to-seven-year loan without payments, but once we explain it to the seller, he usually cooperates.

We just state our position simply and truthfully. We can't buy the house if the seller won't accept our terms; even if we did buy it, we might not be able to hold onto it if the payments were too high. That wouldn't be any better for the seller than it would be for us. He wants to be rid of the house permanently; he doesn't want to foreclose and take it back again a year or two after the sale. That gives him good reason to work with us and do things our way.

Occasionally a property is so good that we will pay full price and give the seller some interest on his third loan besides. In these cases, we try to keep the interest on the third down to a simple 10 percent or less.

Let the Seller Get the Loan

Whenever possible, we have the seller take out the second in his name, and then we take the property subject to that loan. This way there is no liability for us. The loan usually costs less, too, if the seller applies for it instead of the buyer.

Of course, the seller doesn't tell the lender that the house is being sold. He doesn't lie about anything, but he doesn't advertise his personal business, either. The loan is fully assumable anyway, so it is really none of the lender's business.

If the seller can't qualify for the loan, or refuses to do it, we apply for a purchase-money second. Sometimes we tell the lender that there will be a third loan from the seller after their second. Other lenders don't ask, but we never lie to anyone or do anything dishonest, illegal, or unethical.

The institutional lenders are always in second position, ahead of the sellers, so the seller's third lien doesn't affect these lenders. They're protected. Their loan usually covers only up to about 70 percent of the value of the house, so even in a foreclosure the lender wouldn't lose any money.

While we're on the subject of loans, we'd like to add that it's extremely important to meet your obligations. We're very scrupulous about making our payments on time. We've developed a good reputation, and we work hard to maintain it. This is why we're able to get sellers to work with us. They know that we won't leave them holding the bag. *This is important.* You can't do business based on trust unless you prove that you deserve that trust and will live up to it. It's great to make demands on the seller, but you also have to think about what you must do in return. There are no rights without responsibilities. That's an old saying, and a true one.

If you're going to conclude successful deals, once you and the seller agree on terms, you're going to need a good sound purchase agreement. That essential part of buying right to manage right is the subject of our next chapter.

Four

Purchase Agreements

What do you need in a good purchase agreement? What should it cover? How should you work it? What is it all about? What is the purchase agreement designed to do? Have you really thought about it? Have you asked yourself what you want a purchase agreement to do?

To begin with, you want to make sure that everything about your purchase is spelled out in detail. Never ever accept verbal assurances. If the seller is afraid to put it in writing, he probably doesn't intend to follow through with his promises; and even if he is honest, people do forget. If it's all down in black and white, there are no surprises and no arguments when escrow is about to close.

WHO PAYS FOR WHAT?

Some of the items you need to consider when writing your purchase agreement are: Who pays what costs? Does the buyer get the insurance and the tax reserve (impound) accounts, or do they go to the seller? Is the interest simple or compounded? What day are the payments due? You need the names of the buyer and seller, the address of the property, the purchase price, and the terms. The more details you put in, the more secure your agreement will be.

Be specific when you write down those details. People don't feel committed if the agreement is too vague. They want to know what they're agreeing to. The more firmly you nail down the details, the more you involve them in the transaction, and the more involvement they have in it, the less likely they are to change their minds and walk away from the deal.

Of course, you might easily be the one to change your mind and walk away. There are all sorts of reasons for this, and one easy solution: You put a weasel clause into every offer you write.

THE WEASEL, OR ESCAPE, CLAUSE

A weasel clause is anything that will let you weasel out of the purchase and still get your deposit back. You can make the deal contingent upon getting suitable financing. Or you can be more specific than that and say that you'll buy the property only if you can get the second mortgage for 17 percent interest or less, with not more than four points for the loan fee.

You can make the deal contingent on almost anything you can get the seller to go along with—the sale of another property, an appraisal, an engineer's report, your spouse's (attorney's, accountant's, mother-in-law's) approval.

One of the most useful ideas is to make the sale contingent on inspection of the property. This way, you don't even have to look at the property until you know that you can make a deal with the seller. Why should you want to see the house before then? You might not buy it anyway. But once you have the terms worked out, you know that you're at least interested in the house. If you're going to buy a lot of property, you can't afford to look at every house that sounds good. It wastes time, effort, and gasoline. By making your offers contingent on inspection, you can save yourself a lot of wear and tear.

This technique also tells sellers that they're dealing with a professional. It lets them know that their houses are nothing special to you, but just commodities that you trade in as part of your business. More importantly, it helps implant that idea in your own head and encourages you to think of houses as simply part of your business. This is part of the process that helps you become a "don't wanter" buyer.

PERSONALIZED FORMS

As a buyer, you should print up forms of your own that are slanted toward the buyer. In most states standard purchase agreement and contract forms usually contain clauses written to favor the seller. These emphasize the seller's rights and the buyer's responsibilities. This is because these standard forms are written by and for real estate agents, and real estate agents work for the seller. The seller gives them a listing, which is a written contract promising the agents a commission when the house is sold. The buyer has only a verbal agreement with the agent and pays him nothing.

Nowadays, there are buyer's agents. You, as a buyer, can hire someone like this to represent you. You would draw up an agreement with him, separate from the purchase agreement, and agree to pay him either a flat fee or a percentage of the purchase price.

Whether you hire an agent or not, you need a good contract, one with your own clauses in it. This doesn't mean that you tell the seller you want to use your own contract, you just do it. You go to a printer and have your own forms printed up with "Standard Purchase Agreement" printed in bold letters across the top.

This allows you to slant the purchase agreement more in your favor without advertising what you're doing. Why warn the seller that you have things weighted in your favor? Your terms are printed there for him to read and anything written or typed into the contract supersedes anything that is printed, so the seller can still make any sort of change he wants. However, people's faith in the printed word and standard forms increases the chances that sellers will accept your form without making changes. When they read your contract and believe that it's all standard, they will probably assume that it's the way everyone buys and sells property. That way, how can they object to the way you purchase their house? Why should they expect special treatment? (The same technique works very well with notes.)

THE FINANCING

The purchase agreement should spell out all the details of the financing. How much cash do you put down, if any? How much cash does the seller get? Where will it come from? Who pays the points? Will you assume the existing loans, take the property subject to them, or pay them off? How much interest will there be, and how will it be paid? When does the interest start? Will there be monthly payments, or one balloon payment at the end? All this has to be spelled out in the purchase agreement. Negotiating a terrific deal doesn't mean anything until you get it all down on paper and get the seller's signature. And remember, everything is negotiable.

RENT IT OUT BEFORE YOU BUY

How can you rent out a house before you even buy it? As a smart investor-landlord, you have to turn that question around and ask yourself how you can take a chance on buying property before you have it rented. After all, you are buying the house for a rental. If you can't get it rented easily at a good price, you have no reason to buy it. If you close escrow first and then begin your rental campaign, you're taking a big chance. At best, you're going to lose money. Once the escrow closes, you begin making payments. However, with no renter in your property, you'll have no income coming in to meet those payments.

What if the house sits empty for a couple of weeks, or even a couple of months? You're not only losing money each day, but you're leaving yourself open to vandalism. Vacant houses attract trouble. Kids like to break the windows, and vagrants like to sleep inside. Who needs this kind of aggravation? You don't. You have too many other important things to worry about. Also, as a matter of principle and sound business practice, you shouldn't be burdening yourself with responsibilities that belong to the seller.

As a professional landlord-investor, you want to cut your overhead and your hassles to the bone. You don't want to see the houses until you're sure you're going to buy them, and you don't want to commit yourself irrevocably to buying them until you're sure you have them rented out.

This may sound a bit radical at first, but it's actually a simple, straightforward procedure. To begin with, you have to incorporate it into your purchase agreement. Let the sellers know that you're buying their houses for one reason and one reason only: to use them as rentals.

If it turns out a house isn't good for a rental, then you can't use it, and you don't want it. Like the other essential features of your acquisition program, this point is not subject to discussion or compromise.

Proving a house's value as a rental doesn't really put a heavy burden on sellers, anyway. All they have to do is agree to let you advertise and show the house before the close of escrow. You aren't going to let anyone occupy the house before you actually own it, you just want potential tenants to see it. This means that whoever is occupying the house must be cooperative. They must all agree to let prospective tenants come in and look around. If the house is owner-occupied, this should be no problem at all. The owner wants to sell you the house, so he should be willing to put up with a little bit of inconvenience. If he isn't, then he doesn't want to sell badly enough.

If the house is already tenant-occupied, showing the property to new prospective tenants may be a bit more delicate. Unless the old tenants are moving out voluntarily, they may be hostile and resentful. They don't want to lose their home, and they see no reason to help someone else take it away from them.

If they're good tenants, the obvious way to deal with this is to let them stay. What do you gain from forcing them to move and then hunting up new people to rent to? Nothing. The new tenants may even turn out to be bad ones, and where will you be then?

Remember: The key to a successful long-term rental program is tenant stability. If you have a chance to hold on to good tenants who have already been in the house for a while, why not grab it? You'll have to explain to them that their rent will be raised, and you may have to compromise and raise it less than you'd like, but it can still be worth it. Even if doing this raises your negative cash flow a bit, it might be to your advantage to have tenants who are familiar with the house and all its quirks and problems (and therefore won't be demanding all sorts of repairs and improvements), and who want to stay.

Make the Seller Get Rid of Bad Tenants

If the current tenants aren't good, or if their rent is so far below market that a reasonable raise still won't bring it up to a fair rate, it's the seller's problem. He'll have to explain to them that the house is being sold and that they will eventually have to leave. In the meantime, unless they want to leave immediately, they have to cooperate with the new buyer, meaning you.

If they refuse to cooperate, the seller should evict them. Otherwise, he'll pass his problem along to you. It's a big mistake to let him get away with this. If the seller is afraid of his tenants, and you're afraid to stand up to him, you're off to a very bad start. You'll be closing escrow and taking possession of something even worse than a vacant house—one with undesirable tenants. If the seller couldn't get them to show the house or leave, then how are you going to do it? You're going to be stuck with all the hassle and expense of going through the eviction process.

You'll have to hire a lawyer, a process server, and others, and take time out from your other, more profitable activities to go to court. Once the old tenants are gone, you'll have to clean up the house and repaint it, and then wait for a new tenant to come along. All this time, you will be getting little or no income from the property. How long could you go on like that? It wouldn't take many deals like this to put you under.

Set Up a Reasonable Schedule for Showing the Property

On the other hand, you have to be reasonable. You can't really expect anyone, tenant or owner, to put up with a steady stream of people through their house at all hours of the day and night. Set up definite days and times when prospective tenants can view the house. Make sure that people call first for an appointment rather than just charging over, and whenever possible you should try to be there yourself.

In addition, you should always prescreen people before you send them to look at the house. This will cut down on the number of people who bother the current occupants, and it will also eliminate the gawkers and time wasters. Prescreening will make life easier for both you and the current occupants of the house. Ask people questions on the phone. Find out who they are, what they do for a living, how much rent they can pay, whether they have ever been evicted, and so on. You don't even send them to look at the house unless you get the right answers.

See the sample list of clauses for buyers on the facing page.

BUYER'S CLAUSES

1. Seller hereby agrees to furnish a termite inspection and clearance and a roof inspection and clearance both by licensed contractors.

2. Seller to warrant all plumbing, electrical, heating, cooling, and appliances to be in a safe and proper working order at close of escrow. Seller will deliver home clean, vacant, and landscaping well maintained to buyer at close of escrow. All debris to be removed from the yard, and property to be free of any broken windows.

3. This offer is subject to the assigned buyer's inspection and written approval of subject property within 5 days of acceptance of this offer by the seller. A list of repairs necessary will be prepared by the buyer and must be signed by both parties as to who does what work. Said repairs will be accomplished within 5 days before close of escrow and evidenced by final written clearance provided to escrow. Buyer reserves the right to a walk-through inspection and approval 24 hours before closing. All utilities to be on at this time, paid for by the Seller. If repairs are not completed, $1,000 shall be held back in escrow to cover the cost of any incomplete repairs.

4. There shall be no prepayment penalty on the notes created herein.

5. Buyer is purchasing subject property for investment purposes and may rent, lease, resell, or trade subject property.

6. Impound account and Insurance to be transferred to buyer "gratis" at no cost at the option of the Buyer.

7. Offer is subject to _____(name)_____ appraising for a minimum of $_____ Quick sale value.

8. Earnest money to be deposited in escrow upon acceptance of this offer by Seller.

9. Prior to the close of escrow, Seller agrees to show subject property to Buyer's prospective tenants.

10. Seller to furnish Buyer with any rental agreements/leases and tenant information on subject property, subject to Buyer's inspection and written approval.

Five

Constructing an Ad Campaign

How do you attract the right tenants? You advertise. A rental property in search of a tenant is a product you have to market just like any other product. You are competing against every other landlord out there with a property to rent, trying to get those good tenants, who are in short supply. You have to be aggressive and get out there and let those tenants know what you have to offer.

You make your rents attractive by pricing them about $25 below comparable rents for the area. Check with local realtors and check newspaper ads, rental agencies, and other relevant sources to get an idea of what the average rents are for the area if you don't already know. By the time you reach this point in your landlording career you should have a firm idea of what rents are like in the area, so deciding how much to charge shouldn't be a big problem for you. You should also have a good idea of the vacancy rate for houses such as the one you are buying. (Unless the vacancy rate is extremely low, you shouldn't be buying rental property in that area.)

Armed with this knowledge, you should be able to construct an ad campaign that will get the house rented with a minimum of fuss and effort. If you have a strong landlord's market, you may need to put only the property description and price in the ad—for example: "Three-bedroom, two-bath house, Southside, $350 a month" and a phone number. This may be enough to keep your phone ringing off the hook.

ADVERTISING IN A RENTER'S MARKET

If it isn't, you may have to get a little fancy and creative. Think about the things that make the house attractive: access to schools, shopping, transportation, et cetera. Think of any special features the house has: large landscaped yards, garage and carport, fireplace, family room, et cetera. You want to draw attention to any features that will make the house stand out from the others on the market. Get as many of those features as you can into your ad. Let people know that you are offering more than just another house for rent.

Start your ads with a bang! "Spectacular view, large spacious rooms, excellent schools and transportation, growth area for jobs." These are the things people want to know. Once you grab their interest, then you can hit them with the rent, the location, and other details.

Newspapers may not be the best places to advertise, either. Dollar for dollar, newspaper advertising doesn't always deliver the best value anymore; often, radio and television can be cheaper in the long run.

Television

Unfortunately, television advertising is rarely cheap. It's cost-effective only in terms of reaching a large audience. If you have one or two houses to rent, this probably won't be practical. It would be overkill. You'd be paying for far more advertising than you need.

If you're a large landlord, however, you may want to give serious consideration to the idea of using TV. You don't want to take a full-minute prime-time ad on Super Bowl Sunday. What you want is thirty seconds on the smallest, cheapest station. VHF and non-network-affiliated stations are usually your best bet.

Many smaller stations that are hurting for advertising business may even take your ad on a commission or PI (per inquiry) basis. This means that you pay them nothing up front. You either pay them a commission on each property that gets rented, or a fee for each person who responds to the ad and inquires about renting one of your houses.

This probably won't work if you're in a large, prosperous market for TV advertising. For instance, the New York and Los Angeles areas would be too large and expensive. But in the smaller rural or urban markets the local stations may be more than happy to work with you.

Radio

Radio generally covers a smaller area than TV does, and the ads are usually cheaper. The problem with radio is that each station aims at a different audience; it is a highly specialized medium. Either you have to identify with the specific group of renters you are aiming at and then find the radio station that caters to that group, or you have to find the station that has the largest mass appeal.

More homework. More research to do. The thing that makes it worthwhile is that radio can reach the people you want. Many of those people don't read the newspapers. That's right. They don't read newspapers, so they might not even see your ad. But everyone listens to the radio and/or watches television.

You'll be hitting them with a new idea, one that they aren't expecting, and one that your competition hasn't caught on to yet. The early bird gets the worm, and the first landlord to come up with a new advertising twist gets the cream of the tenant crop. The rest of the landlords get what's left over.

Flyers

If you can't afford radio or television, you can still find some other new and innovative ways to advertise your vacancies. Try flyers. You can get them printed and distributed relatively cheaply, and it's a great way to target a certain area or group of people.

You can hire students or unemployed people to carry flyers door-to-door in a housing tract. Even if no one who lives there is interested in moving, some of them may know someone who is. Many times people have a friend or relative who would like to live near them. By letting these people know that you have one or more vacancies, you can be doing a favor for them and for yourself, too. (Naturally, you instruct your distributors to leave flyers only at the well-kept houses in desirable rental areas.)

You should be able to get a thousand flyers printed and passed out door-to-door for under fifty dollars. The response may not be immediate, but if you do this every time you have a vacancy, you'll gradually make an impact. Eventually you could become so well known as a local landlord that people will call you when they want to find a house to rent, or even when they have a home they want to sell.

Telephone poles, billboards, and bulletin boards in supermarkets, laundromats, and other public places are also good spots to advertise. You can also try hitting people where they work. Many factories have areas where workers and others can put up notices. This can be an excellent way to reach the people you want—people who are steadily employed and who want to live near their jobs.

Flyers also give you another advantage. You can say a lot more about the property on a flyer than you can in an advertisement. You aren't paying by the letter, the word, or the line, so you are no longer compelled to be as brief as possible. You can go into detail and let people know what they'll be renting. You can go on about the number and size of the rooms, the carpeting, and so on. If you are willing to accept some pets but not others, you have a chance to explain that. If you want to offer alternatives and options to potential tenants, you have the space to explain those.

The drawback to flyers is that you're not going to be hitting the people who are specifically looking for houses to rent. This is the big advantage of newspaper advertising: Your ad is put specifically in the "Homes for Rent" section, where, presumably, everyone who reads it will be a potential tenant.

Military Newspapers

We've found that the local military newspaper is a good place to advertise. There's a big Air Force base in Tucson, and we find that Air Force people make excellent tenants, because they know how to follow rules and have steady employment.

So there are your basic choices: General-interest newspapers hit the large, targeted audience, but they are expensive and miss a lot of people who don't read newspapers. Plus, you have to be concise. Radio is too specialized and probably too expensive if you're just a small landlord. And flyers don't reach enough people.

Which one do you choose? Maybe you should try the shotgun approach and use all the media at once. Or you can use one or two of these methods. It all depends on your situation, the size of your operation, the nature of the rental market in your area, and your own personality.

Once you have your rental program going well, and have several tenants, you might want to try the following technique to fill vacancies.

FINDER'S FEES

Tenant incentive programs can locate good tenants and entice them into your homes. For example, we offer our tenants a $25 bonus if they refer other tenants to us. This way we get pre-screened tenants who have been recommended to us and who know what our program is all about and how it works. It saves us time, money, and effort; we spend less on advertising and have our houses vacant for less time.

CONSTRUCTING YOUR AD

What do you want to put in your rental ads? Think about what will attract people. What was important when you were looking at the house as a potential buyer? What did you assume tenants would be looking for? That's what you want to emphasize in your ads. The garage, the backyard, the family room, the privacy—these are the things that prospective tenants are looking for. Advertise them; let people know that you have what they want.

Ideally, you want to write ads that will attract tenants to your overall program, not just to one particular property. Let them know that all your houses are in good, livable condition. Let them know that you rent only houses with two bathrooms and backyards. If you're going to buy and hold a lot of property, you can't afford to advertise every house individually.

Does a doctor advertise for patients one at a time? Do lawyers advertise case by case? Does Chevrolet try to sell each one of its cars individually? You have to start thinking big. You're in the landlord business, and you want people to know that. You want them to think of you when they need a place to rent.

Here's an example of the sort of ad we run frequently in Tucson:

DISCOUNT RENT

Fantastic 3-bedroom, 2-bath house in Sahuaro area. Fenced, new kitchen. $425 Discount Rent 748-1010.

HOW DISCOUNT RENT WORKS:

Actual Rent	$475
Discount Rent	$425

$50 DISCOUNT ONLY:
1. Make rent payment on or before the first of each month' and
2. Tenant takes care of all minor maintenance—$50 Deductible program.

That ad describes exactly how the Discount Rent Program works. Actually, in the above market rent for similar houses is about $450. The tenants are still getting a $25 discount, though. And the savings to us in time, money, and aggravation is certainly worth $25 a month for each house in our Discount Program. (We'll explain this more in the next chapter.)

You'll notice that the ad mentions the rent has to be paid on or before the first of the month, and the tenant is responsible for *all* minor maintenance. We mean it, and we let the tenants know we mean it. The first time they're late with their rent, or the first time they ask us to take care of some small repair, they owe us $50.

No one seems bothered by that rule, though. Every time we run that ad, our phone rings off the hook because so many people want to get into our Discount Rent Program.

You may not want to run an ad just like ours, and you probably won't advertise every week, but you do want to become well known for what you do. Remember, you're proud of what you do, and you're in the rental business to stay. Let people know that. Ideally, you want to reach a point where you won't have to advertise even when you have vacancies. People will know about you and what you do, and you'll have a waiting list.

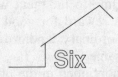

Six

Picking the Right Tenants

A young man wanted to rent a house from us. He had no credit history and no steady income, but he explained this by saying he had just gotten out of the military and was going to school on the GI Bill. He needed a place to live right away and I guess he thought we would take pity on an ex-soldier.

Now, we're as patriotic as anyone and we have a lot of military personnel as tenants. Generally, we've found them to be reliable and trustworthy, but we still have our rules. We told the young man he would have to fill out an application and then be interviewed, just like anyone else. It would take at least a week or more, while we checked with his ex-commanding officer and other references. He stormed out and we never heard from him again, but we didn't cry. If he was honest he should have been willing and able to play by the rules—especially if he just got out of the military.

ALWAYS PICK YOUR TENANTS—NEVER LET THEM PICK YOU

We believe it's up to you to pick your tenants, rather than letting your tenants pick you. Whenever possible, interview them on the phone before you meet them face-to-face. Find out if they're the kind of people you want. Tell them a little bit about your program and what you expect from your tenants. This is an excellent time to hit them with the idea of discount rent programs as a reward for good tenants. Let them know that you aren't the ordinary landlord who treats all tenants—good and bad—the same.

As we mentioned in the previous chapter, the Discount Rent Program is just what it sounds like. You set your rent at or slightly above the normal market rate. Then you give the tenants a discount of $50 to $75 if they follow all your rules. For example, you might determine that $350 is the average rent for houses like yours. Therefore, you set your rent at $375, and offer the tenants a $50 discount if they pay their rent on time and take care of minor maintenance. This means that they would actually end up paying only $325 per month, which is $25 less than the market average for the area.

This is a good idea for the good tenant who intends to pay his rent on time and doesn't mind fixing things. He can save $25 a month and get a good house to rent besides. But the bad tenant, the guy who pays late and counts on you to fix everything, will lose out. Every time his rent is late, he pays $375 a month instead of $325. Every time he picks up the phone to bother you with some minor problem, it costs him $50, so your program has only disadvantages for him.

Getting this information across on the phone can save you time and aggravation later. Why waste time and energy meeting with people you don't want to rent to? The more shortcuts you can develop, the more smoothly your program will run. This means that you never invest any time in people until you know it's worth your while to do so.

Ask as many questions on the phone as you can. Answer as many of their questions as you can. This is what the telephone is for. It puts distance between you and the person you're talking to. If they don't sound right, one little click will quickly end the discussion.

While you have people on the phone, find out whom you're talking to. What do they do for a living? How long have they been employed there? How many people in the family? How many children? How many pets? What kinds of pets do they have? Where are they living now? How long have they been there? Why are they moving? What type of housing are they used to? Will your house be a move up for them, or a move down?

It's like a game of cat and mouse. Enjoy it at this point. Don't take it too seriously, because you have nothing to lose. If you don't like their answers, you don't tell them where the house is located. The location is your secret, and they have to pry it out of you. Don't make it too easy on them. If you think it's hard getting a good tenant into your property, think about what it could be like trying to get a bad tenant out.

MEETING THE APPLICANTS

Once you've decided to let someone see the house, make him come to you. The more effort prospective tenants put into trying to view the house, the more they should appreciate it once they do. If the house is occupied, they can call for an appointment, or you can do it for them. If the house is empty, they have to come to your office to get the key.

Never offer to meet them at the house and show it to them personally. This is investing too much time and effort before you know if it's worthwhile. It lets the tenant know that you care too much about getting the property rented, so you get off on the wrong foot with them.

Instead, you will let the applicants stop by and pick up a key so that they can go show themselves the house. Naturally, you aren't going to simply hand out keys to everyone who comes along and then hope you get all the keys back. We ask people to sign a key agreement like the one on page 87 and leave a $25 deposit.

If the people don't have $25, you could probably ask them for a driver's license, or perhaps a credit card or something else of value. We feel that the kinds of tenants we want should be able to come up with $25 if they're out looking for a house to live in. However, the decision is yours. The main point is to have them deposit something they want back, so that they'll return the keys to your office.

If you don't have an office, create one. Don't have them come to your house; you want to keep your personal life and your business completely separate. You never want tenants or prospective tenants to know where you live, or you'll be constantly facing them and all their problems right at your doorstep.

Also, if they don't know where you live, they don't know how far you have to travel to meet them. One highly successful landlord we know finds out where the prospective tenants are located, then says he is clear across town and suggests they meet somewhere in between as a compromise. Just by coincidence, the compromise location is usually within a block or two of the landlord's home, while the prospective tenant has to travel a good distance.

You can't do this, however, unless you have a good strong key agreement, such as the sample on the facing page, to protect you and make it clear that the prospective tenant has permission only to inspect the house, not to move in.

CREATING YOUR OWN OFFICE

Another favorite technique for dealing with tenants is to make yourself look important. If you don't have an office, make people think you do. If you ask a tenant if he's familiar with a certain well-known bank or office building and he says yes, then say, "Fine—I'll meet you down in the main lobby." If he isn't familiar with it, give him directions on how to get there.

This way, while you're not lying or saying anything deliberately misleading, you're creating the impression that you have an office in a building. "I'll meet you down in the main lobby" sounds like you're coming from somewhere upstairs. (Just make sure you pick a building with more than one floor!)

The problem with this approach is simple. How does the tenant return the key? Do you meet him back at the same spot in two hours? Do you have him call you when he's ready to return it? Do you give him a stamped, self-addressed envelope and let him mail it back to you? What do you do if he comes looking for you and can't find your office in the bank building?

This is why many landlords prefer the coffee-shop routine. They tell tenants to meet them at their office, the ABC Coffee Shop. This way, they can sit around and wait in comfort. If the

KEY AGREEMENT

I, the undersigned, hereby acknowledge the acceptance of a key to a house located at _____(address)_____ in the city of ___(Tucson)___, state of ___(Arizona)___. I have paid the required deposit of $25 (twenty-five) dollars and agree to meet the following conditions:

1. To pick up the key from this office and leave CASH or CHECK deposit of $25 (twenty-five) dollars.
2. To bring the key back within 2 (two) hours of departure from this office.

I understand that the failure to return the key within the time specified will result in the owner changing the locks. I understand the deposit will be used to pay for the expense of changing the locks on the above-named house.

I fully understand and agree to all of the above.

_____   _____
Signature   Time Left

_____   _____
Date   Time Due

prospective tenant likes the house, they can conduct their rental interview there, too. It creates a nice relaxed atmosphere, but it's still impersonal. It's a public place. If you decide not to rent to a tenant and turn him down, it makes it harder for him to make a scene. You say good-bye, walk away, and that's the end of it.

We don't use or even approve of this idea, but one successful landlord we know even sticks the losers with the check. If he interviews someone he doesn't want to rent to, he excuses himself to go to the men's room and never returns. Since the prospective tenant doesn't know where this landlord lives, the renter is stuck. We feel that tactics like this are harmful and give all landlords a bad name. There is plenty of money to be made legally and morally without resorting to doing things this way.

THE RENTER'S CONVENTION

Another way to get your house rented with a minimum of time and effort on your part is to hold a convention. Rather than setting individual appointments at times convenient for the prospective tenants, just set up one viewing time that is convenient for you and let all your prospective tenants show up at once.

It won't do you any harm to have them competing against each other. People always want something more when they know someone else wants it, too. This is just human nature, so why not take full advantage of it?

DISCRIMINATION IS BAD BUSINESS

One thing you don't want to do, though, is discriminate. Discrimination is not only illegal and morally repugnant: it's not good business. It's just plain stupid to turn someone down because of race, age, sex, or religion. Senseless discrimination hurts you as the landlord. It limits your access to the supply of good tenants, who come in all colors, ages, religions, and nationalities. If you're guided by prejudice you only make things harder for yourself, even if you don't get caught.

If you do get caught practicing discrimination, you can be in a lot of trouble: you can be sued for damages and fined heavily. There are all sorts of laws against discrimination, and they call for civil and criminal penalties. You can't run your rental properties and go to court every day at the same time. So, please, stay out of trouble and judge people by who they are, not what they look like and how they worship.

Turning away tenants because you don't like who they are or what they do for a living is another matter. It not only makes sense to protect yourself, it's legal.

A couple of years ago, a single black woman in New York put in an application to rent an apartment and was turned down. She then sued the landlord. Her suit charged the landlord with discrimination on the basis of race and sex.

The landlord claimed he was innocent. He said that he didn't care that she was black, and he didn't care that she was a woman. He turned her down because she was a lawyer. The man admitted that he was prejudiced against lawyers. He felt that they were likely to be argumentative, troublesome tenants. He had many black tenants and female tenants, but he did not rent to lawyers.

The judge ruled in the landlord's favor. He said that as long as the landlord was not discriminating on the basis of race or sex, he had a right to protect his interests. Since educated people, particularly lawyers, might be more aware of their rights, they could be considered troublesome tenants.

GET TO KNOW RENTERS

So how do you find out who people are and what they're like? You talk to them and ask them questions. Find out where they work, and why. Do they like it? Will they be staying?

Once you know they want the house, *always* have them fill out a credit application and pay you a credit-check fee before you go any further. If you don't belong to a local credit reporting service, join one right away. The credit check will tell you a lot about people. People with unhealthy credit histories usually won't make good tenants. And the more elaborate their explanation, the more likely it is that they'll be trouble.

Listen to these people when you talk to them. Ask them questions, and then listen some more. Ask them why they want to rent the house. Why do they want to be in that particular part of town? The normal people will give you normal answers. They'll tell you about the school their children can walk to, their jobs, or friends or relatives who don't live too far away.

People who give you long, involved, strange stories are the ones you want to stay away from. If their lives are in turmoil and/or they have a hard time paying their bills, what makes you think you will get your rent? Use your common sense and trust your own judgment if someone just doesn't seem right.

A woman once turned in an application to us, and neither of us felt good about her. Her credit wasn't excellent, but it wasn't bad. There was something else about her, and we just weren't sure what we should do. Then our office manager took us aside and told us not to rent to her. The woman had been a neighbor of the office manager's parents. Her baby had burned in a fire. Another child had been taken away from her, and she had been married seven times. Obviously, a woman like this has problems. We are landlords, not social workers. We didn't rent to her.

In order to find out if you want them as tenants, you have to spend time with people before you rent to them. You talk to them on the phone, then you let them come and get a key and fill out a credit application. Then, if their credit checks out, you put them through the rental interview. This is when you really grill them.

You should figure on spending at least an hour and a half on the interview. This is important for numerous reasons. It gives you a chance to just be around the prospective tenants for a while. See how you feel about that. Do they seem normal? Do they seem strange?

Watch them. See how they act toward each other and toward you over the extended period of time. Do they seem stable, peaceful, and responsible? Do they seem as though they will take care of your property?

You can't decide these things in five minutes. You have to take your time. There are no effective shortcuts. Would you give someone the keys to your car if you didn't know them well? What is your car worth? Eight thousand dollars? Ten thousand dollars? What is a rental house worth? Personally, we wouldn't dream of turning over an asset that's worth $40,000 to $80,000 to a family of total strangers.

If you can't spend time interviewing tenants before you rent to them, how are you going to find time to evict the bad ones later? How are you going to find time to repair the damage they do, or to find new tenants to rent to? If you are too busy to interview tenants thoroughly, then you are too busy to own rentals and manage them yourself.

Make Your Rules Clear

During the rental interview, go over your rental agreement line by line. You must keep emphasizing how tough you are and how hard and how quickly you come down on tenants who break the rules.

The first thing a prospective tenant sees when he walks into our office is our office manager. Her desk is positioned in the hallway so that she can intercept people as they come in the door. On her desk is a big sign facing the door. The sign says: "Pay Your Rent On Time." Applicants can't miss it. After they have the rules, she keeps them seated in her office/reception area while they fill out the key deposit form and/or the credit application and rental application.

This way, our message really sinks in. Every time they look up, the sign is staring them in the face. They get the idea that this rule is important to us. If we don't get our rent, bad things will happen, all of them perfectly legal, but all of them fairly unpleasant. The backslider's credit will be shot. They will be evicted, if necessary. Their names will get around to other landlords, and no one will want to rent to them.

None of these possibilities will scare away the honest renter. Good people will try twice as hard to prove to you that they deserve to rent your house. It's only the professional deadbeat who is already thinking about what will happen when, not if, he doesn't pay his rent. The honest person has no reason to fear your penalties; he isn't going to break the rules. He intends to pay his rent on time, so he isn't concerned about the penalties, only the rewards.

So now we go into the actual interview. But first, look through the sample rental application and employment verification and credit check forms. They are what the interview is all about.

RENTAL APPLICATION

Prospective Address _____ Desired Date of Occupancy _____

Desired Length of Occupancy _____

Tenant_____ Social Security # _____

Date of Birth_____ Mother's Maiden Name_____

Present Address_____ How Long?_____

City_____ State_____ Zip Code_____

Phone_____ Why are you moving?_____

Landlord_____ Phone_____

Previous Address_____ How Long?_____

City_____ State_____ Zip Code_____

Driver's License #_____

Type of Car_____ License #_____

Employer's Name_____ Phone_____

Address_____ Position_____

How Long?_____ Your Superior_____

Monthly Income   Source [   ] wages   [   ] commission   [   ] gov't assistance

Take-home Pay_____   [   ] salary   [   ] tips   [   ] other_____

Previous Employer_____ How Long?_____

Military

Branch_____ Rank_____ ID#_____

Discharge Date_____ Station_____

Cotenant_____ Social Security #_____

Date of Birth_____ Mother's Maiden Name_____

Relation to Tenant_____ Driver's License #_____

Employer's Name_____ Phone_____

Address_____ Position_____

How Long?_____ Your Superior_____

Monthly Income   Source [   ] wages   [   ] commission   [   ] gov't assistance

Take-home Pay_____   [   ] salary   [   ] tips   [   ] other_____

Other Tenants   Age   Relationship   Occupation

_____

_____

_____

Learned Skills

[   ] Plumbing   [   ] Electrical   [   ] Cement Work

[   ] Roofing   [   ] Painting   [   ] Auto Mechanics

[   ] Appliance Repair (type)   [   ] Carpentry   [   ] Other _____

RENTAL APPLICATION (continued)

Pet Name	Type/Breed	Size	Sex	Indoor/Outdoor
1.				
2.				

Credit References	Address	Limit	Purpose	Acct. Open?
1.				
2.				
3.				
4.				

Personal References	Address	City/State/Zip	Phone
1.			
2.			

Nearest Relative	Address	City/State/Zip	Phone
1.			

Banks	Account #	Checking/Savings	Branch
1.			
2.			

Visa/Mastercard	Account #	Issuing Bank	Limit
1.			
2.			

Do you own any real estate?   [ ] Yes [ ] No
If so, where and what?_____
Have you ever been evicted from any tenancy?   [ ]yes [ ]no
Have you ever willfully and intentionally refused to pay rent when due?   [ ]yes [ ]no
Do you know of anything which may interrupt income or ability to pay rent? [ ]yes [ ]no

   I hereby certify that the answers I have given in this application are true and correct to the best of my knowledge. I understand that any false answers or statements made by me will be sufficient grounds for eviction and loss of any security deposit.
   Applicant permits and agrees to pay a fee of $7.50 for a credit check to be performed on himself and his co-occupant by his signature below:

_____   _____   _____
Date   Tenant   Cotenant

Discrimination
It is against the law to discriminate against tenants on the basis of race, religion, national origin, age, or neighborhood racial makeup.

EMPLOYMENT VERIFICATION INQUIRY LETTER

April 4, 1983

(Employer's name)
(Employer's address)
(Employer's city, state, zip)

REFERENCE: (Name of Prospective Tenant)

Dear Sir:

  (Name of prospective tenant) has given me your name as
his employer on an application to rent a dwelling located
at (address of your property, city, state, zip).
  He claims his job position is (give his job title), that
his salary is $ (figure given you) per (week or month), and
that he has worked for you from (starting date) to the
present.
  Please supply the following information by phone or
detach the bottom section of this letter and return it to
me. My phone number is 748-1010. The best time to reach me
is (give times).
  Thank you for your cooperation.

                         Sincerely yours,

                         Michael J. Milin

MJM/jea

- -

  1. Is he currently your employee? ___Yes ___No
  2. What is his job title? _____
  3. What is his salary? $_____ per week__ month__
  4. How long has he worked for you? _____

_____ _____ _____
Name   Title   Date

CREDIT CHECK INQUIRY LETTER

April 4, 1983

(Creditor's name)
(Creditor's address)
(Creditor's city, state, zip)

REFERENCE: (Name of Prospective Tenant)

Dear Sir:

(Name of prospective tenant) has given me your name as a credit reference on an application to rent a dwelling located at (address of your property, city, state, zip).

He claims he has a loan or bill outstanding with you in the amount of $ (figure given you) and that his payments are $ (figure given you) per month.

Please supply the following information by phone or detach the bottom section of this letter and return it to me. My phone number is 748-1010. The best time to reach me is (give times).

Thank you for your cooperation.

Sincerely yours,

Michael J. Milin

MJM/jea

- -

1. How much does he owe you? _____
2. What are his payments per month? _____
3. Is he current or delinquent in his payments? _____
4. What is his paying history? _____

_____   _____   _____
Name   Title   Date

DEPOSIT TO RESERVE HOUSE

Name _____

Phone_____ Rental Address _____

The undersigned has hereby given a deposit in the amount of Two Hundred Dollars ($200) to reserve the dwelling located at the above address for possible owner consideration of acceptance for rental.

If prospective tenant is declined residency for any reason whatsoever, deposit is fully refundable.

In the event prospective tenant changes his/her mind about renting, deposit is NONREFUNDABLE.

I fully understand the above statements and agree to abide by them.

_____   _____
Tenant   Cotenant

_____   _____
Witness   Date

Seven

The Rental Interview

By the time tenants come to our office for the interview they know better than to take us lightly and they know who is in control. We never put ourselves in a position where we are so desperate to rent a house that we will take anybody who calls or shows up. People have to pass through our screening process before they ever get to the interview, because that's just the final step. By then, we already know that their references and credit check out and that we want to rent to them.

Up until this point, we invest almost no time in people who apply to rent our homes. Why should we? First of all, we're busy people. If we spent all our time interviewing prospective tenants and weeding out the undesirables, we would have no time to do all the other things that busy property owners need to do, and no time for a personal life, either.

More importantly, we might be pushed into making bad decisions. Once you do invest time in a prospect, it becomes harder to turn him down. You think about all that time you spent, and you hate to see it go to waste. You start rationalizing and finding reasons why this applicant isn't so bad, even if you know he is. Experienced landlords who should know better get caught in this trap all the time. In most cases they're sorry afterward, but people in tight spots sometimes do foolish things.

This is why we keep our distance and let the rental process run by itself, like a machine. The prospects come to our office with a key deposit in hand, or they gather at our tenants' conventions. Either way, we eyeball them first and make them audition for us before we ever get around to inviting one of them in for an interview. And the interview is strictly by our invitation.

WE'RE TOUGH INTERVIEWERS

Once we do invite a tenant to meet with us, we get serious. From then on, we put time and energy into dealing with the prospect—a lot of time and energy. When it gets down to this point, we're ready to get personally involved in the screening process.

We treat the tenant interview like a job interview. We are the employers, and the people we're interviewing are applying for the job of tenants. It's a job with specific requirements and responsibilities, and that's why we're so careful about whom we select. We let the applicants know this. They're special people, the cream of the crop. Otherwise, they never would have been chosen for an interview. This is why we expect a lot from them.

We believe renting from us is a privilege and it's not granted to everyone. The lucky few have to earn it. We give them a lot of privileges, and we expect something from them in return. We expect them to be better-than-average tenants who will pay their rent on time and maintain our property for us.

Never Make Exceptions

We have a smoothly functioning system, and we aren't about to change it for anyone. Does General Motors reorganize and/or change its corporate policies every time a new employee is hired? Of course not, and neither do we. Once people understand that, we usually get along. We present our system as though it were a force of nature, or an impersonal machine. It makes no sense to stand up to a tornado or to stick your arm into a jet engine, and it makes no more sense to interfere with our nice, smooth-running system. If a tenant does, we have to fire him.

SETTING THE STAGE

We have a large picture of an eagle on the wall of our office reception area. It's a symbol we adopted from Jack Miller. It stares down at the prospective tenants, aloof and hard-eyed, strong and silent. This is to suggest that we watch over our properties with an eagle eye and protect our houses with the ferocity of an eagle defending its nest. We're absentee landlords, but not absentminded landlords. We're in touch with our properties and on top of what's happening with them even when we're out of town.

If we happen to be away, that doesn't mean it's vacation time for our tenants and that they can stop paying their rent, or send it in late. We wouldn't have much of a system going if we allowed that. We couldn't manage nearly one hundred houses in Arizona and California and still lecture and teach seminars all around the country at the same time.

Every step of our screening process is designed to reinforce this idea in the prospective tenants' minds. Once they've cooled their heels in the reception area for a few minutes under the eagle's watchful gaze, we invite them into our conference room for the rental interview. This helps reinforce the seriousness of the situation. No one just walks in and rents one of our properties. All prospects have to run an obstacle course first, and the interview is the last and hardest obstacle they have to face.

When they get inside the conference room, they're confronted with more signs and reminders. Some of these say: "Pay Your Rent On Time," "Cleanliness Is Next to Godliness," and "If It Wasn't for Landlords, Tenants Would All Be Living in the Streets." These are the first things they see all around them.

Then we come in, sit down with a cup of coffee and make ourselves comfortable for a good long stay. We have a saying in our office: "The rental interview is the cheapest eviction you will ever do." The interview is our last chance to weed out bad tenants before they move into the property. We aren't about to rush it.

ACCENTUATE THE NEGATIVE

We explain to the tenants that we are about to go over the rental agreement, and we explain to them exactly what that means. It's important that they understand that they're signing a legally binding contract that will be enforced. We explain to them that we do our best to uphold our agreement. We are responsible landlords and, therefore, we expect them to be good responsible tenants. If they do what we expect of them, we reward them. If they don't, we punish them. This is no secret. We want all our prospective tenants to know that this is our policy, but we stress the punishment first, and only afterward do we explain the rewards.

Why do we stress the negative side of our program? We do it to scare away the deadbeats. Our screening process is fairly thorough, but every once in a while a deadbeat manages to slip through. Fortunately, we usually catch these in the interview. With all the properties we own, we've had only three evictions in all the years we've been landlording. We have had tenants leave because we couldn't get along with them, but they almost always pay up all they owe and leave the house in good condition. Why? Because they know we won't allow them to do anything else.

Good tenants aren't scared off by our tough penalties. They have no intention of breaking the rules, so they know they won't be penalized. The penalties just don't apply to them. Anyone who does get worried about the penalties is probably not the type of person we want, anyway.

We explain all this to the tenants, and then we explain to them how busy we are. We lecture all across the country and buy properties to sell to investors. Dealing with problem tenants or tenants' problems just isn't on our agenda. Anyone who wants to work for our company as a tenant-manager has to be self-reliant and dependable.

We give applicants a vivid picture of what happens to people who cross us. First we tell them about our record of good tenant relations, but then we tell them about our three evictions—in detail. We explain what happened to the three people who broke their rental agreements with us, and discuss how those people's wages were garnisheed and their credit ratings ruined. It's a sad litany of scary stories with a clear message: If you don't want to follow our rules, don't rent from us.

Telling this to people is one thing; explaining it to them specifically and graphically is something else. This is why we go through the rental agreement with each and every potential tenant, line by line, to be sure that they fully understand what they're agreeing to.

We're very proud of our rental agreement. It took us a long time and a lot of hard experience to develop it and make it work. We feel it's one of the most complete and comprehensive agreements we have seen. It's one of the main reasons our program works so smoothly, so we're going to go through it now, just the way we would for a prospective tenant, and show you how and why it works. First, we suggest you read the agreement in its entirety (pages 103–10) and then we'll analyze what you've read.

EXPLAINING THE RENTAL CONTRACT TO TENANTS

Okay, now that you've read the contract, we can get down to the fun part. Letting tenants read the contract on their own, as you've just done, is not enough. We learned that the hard way, just as we have had to learn a lot of other things. We like to think of ourselves as brilliant and innovative, but not all our ideas have come to us as sudden inspirations or revelations. Many of them have come to us through hard experience, and this matter of making sure tenants understand our agreement is definitely one of them.

We once let a couple of prospective tenants take our rental agreement home with them. They said they had some questions about it and wanted to reread it and think it over. We should have taken the hint and terminated the rental interview right then and there. But this was when our program was just getting started, and we didn't know any better. We never heard from those prospective tenants again, but a few days later, we did get a phone call from the city attorney. She wanted to talk to us about our rental agreement and what was wrong with it. She told

---

RENTAL AGREEMENT

NEW WEST INVESTMENT AND MANAGEMENT
1609 N. Wilmot #104C

Tucson, Arizona 85712   Monday–Friday

(602) 748-1010   10:00 A.M.–5:00 P.M.

THIS AGREEMENT made this ___ day of _____, 19___, by and between _____, herein called "Landlord," and_____, herein called "Tenant." Landlord hereby agrees to rent to Tenant the real property located in the City of _____, County of _____, State of _____, described as follows:_____

commencing on the ___ day of _____ 19___, and monthly thereafter until the first day of _____ 19___, at which time this agreement is terminated. Landlord rents the demised premises to Tenant on the following terms and conditions:

1. Rent
Tenant agrees to pay Landlord as base rent the sum of $___ $450 ___ per month, due and payable monthly in advance on the first day of each month during the term of this agreement. Rent must be received by 5:00 P.M. If the rent has not been received by 9:00 A.M. on the second of the month, then a seven- (7-) day notice will be posted.

2. Payment of Rent
The initial payment of rent and security deposit under the terms of this Rental Agreement must be made in cash. Thereafter monthly rent payments may be paid by check until the first is dishonored and returned unpaid. Time is of the essence and no excuses will be accepted. Rent shall be made payable to _____ _____ and delivered to Landlord at 1609 N. Wilmot #104C, Tucson, AZ 85712 or sent by mail at Tenant's risk to: P.O. Box 17624, Tucson, AZ 85731. Any rents lost in the mail will be treated as if unpaid until received by Owner.

3. Discount Program
As an incentive to the Tenant to pay his rent payments AHEAD OF TIME, and for being responsible for all minor maintenance and repairs (up to $50 in any one month) , a discount in the amount of $50 may be deducted from the above rental sum each month. This discount will automatically be forfeited if the Tenant fails to perform as stated above.

4. Appliances
The house is rented without appliances. The above rental payment specifically EXCLUDES all appliances of any kind! Such appliances as are in the property are there solely at the convenience of the Landlord, who assumes no responsibility for their operation. Landlord agrees to remove appliances at the request of Tenant.

5. Rental Collection Charge
Tenant hereby acknowledges that late payment will cause Landlord to incur costs not contemplated by this Rental Agreement, the exact amount of which will be extremely difficult to ascertain. In the event rent is not received prior to 5:00 P.M. on the 5th of the month, regardless of cause including dishonored checks, Tenant further agrees to pay a late charge to Landlord equal to five percent (5%) of such overdue

RENTAL AGREEMENT (continued)

amount. Neither ill health, loss of job, financial emergency or other excuse will be accepted for late payment.

6. Bad-Check Servicing Charge

In the event Tenant's check is dishonored and returned unpaid for any reason to Landlord, Tenant agrees to pay as additional rental the sum equal to five percent (5%) of the monthly rent. If for any reason a check is returned or dishonored, all future rent payments will be cash or money order.

7. Use

The Tenants agree to use the premises only as a residence for themselves and their children named _____ and their _____ pets named _____. Resident agrees to pay $75 each month for each additional person who shall occupy the premises in any capacity. If Tenants fail to inform Landlord of additional people occupying property, the $75 per person per month fee will be assessed retroactive to the date commencing this Rental Agreement.

8. Pets

There shall be no pets allowed on the rented premises except as may be granted by Landlord, in writing. Tenant hereby agrees that if found in violation, the rents due hereunder may be raised at the Landlord's discretion. If pets are allowed by Landlord, Tenant agrees to render an additional security deposit of $_____.

This consent constitutes a representation by the Tenant and a consent by the Landlord for maintenance in house at said property, of the following described pet:

The animal is a _____ .
The breed is _____ .
The weight is not more than _____ pounds.
The height is not more than _____ inches.
The color is _____ .
Its name is _____ .

The tenant is to be fully responsible for any damage to property of Owner or of others which may result from the maintenance of the pet. Tenants agree to pay for pest infestation services after termination of occupancy. Said monies shall be the responsibility of the Tenant and shall be deducted from the Security Deposit.

Landlord reserves the right to revoke this consent on three days' notice to Tenant, if in the opinion of Landlord's employees, the pet has been a nuisance to other residents or has not been maintained according to these rules. In the event consent is revoked, Tenant agrees to forthwith discontinue maintenance of the pet, and failure to so discontinue shall be a breach of the Rental Agreement. Any animals on the property not registered under this Rental Agreement will be presumed to be strays and will be disposed of according to law, at the option of the Landlord.

9. Nonassignment of Rental Agreement

Resident agrees not to Assign this agreement, nor to Sub-Let any part of the property, nor to allow any other person to live therein other than as named in Paragraph 7 above without first requesting permission from the Owner and paying the appropriate surcharge. Further, that covenants contained in this Rental Agreement, once breached, cannot afterward be performed; and that unlawful detainer proceedings may be commenced.

RENTAL AGREEMENT (continued)

10. Legal Obligations
Tenants hereby acknowledge that they have a legal obligation to pay their rent on time each and every month regardless of any other debts or responsibilities they may have. They agree that they will be fully liable for any back rent owed. They also acknowledge that defaulting on this Rental Agreement could result in a judgment being filed against them and a lien being filed against their current and future assets and/or earnings.

11. Attorney's Cost
If court action is sought by either party to enforce the provisions of the Rental Agreement, attorney's fees and costs may be awarded to the prevailing party in the court action.

12. Repair Policy
The Tenants hereby acknowledge that they have been informed that the Landlord and/or his agents are not always available to provide support services to Tenants. The rental discount is offered for this reason, to encourage tenants to take care of themselves and the property. If a problem comes up that should cost $50 or more to repair, then the Tenants must get in touch with Landlord as soon as possible, between 9:00 A.M. and 5:00 P.M. on Monday through Friday. After normal business hours, tenants may leave a message and someone will get back to them as soon as possible. Under no circumstances will Landlord be responsible for any improvements or repairs costing more than $50 unless the Tenants were given written authorization to make repairs or improvements in advance.

13. Arizona Statutes
To meet all Resident's obligations as spelled out in Section 33-1341, Arizona Statutes, including:

33-1341.   Tenant to Maintain dwelling unit.

1. Comply with all obligations primarily imposed upon tenants by applicable provisions of building codes materially affecting health and safety.
2. Keep that part of the premises that he occupies and uses as clean and safe as the condition of the premises permit.
3. Dispose from his dwelling unit all ashes, rubbish, garbage, and other waste in a clean and safe manner.
4. Keep all plumbing fixtures in the dwelling unit or used by the tenant as clean as their condition permits.
5. Use in a reasonable manner all electrical, plumbing, sanitary, heating, ventilating, air-conditioning, and other facilities and appliances including elevators in the premises.
6. Not deliberately or negligently destroy, deface, damage, impair, or remove any part of the premises or knowingly permit any person to do so.
7. Conduct himself and require other persons on the premises with his consent to conduct themselves in a manner that will not disturb his neighbor's peaceful enjoyment of the premises.

Resident warrants that he/she will meet above conditions in every respect, and acknowledges that failure to perform the obligations herein stipulated will be

RENTAL AGREEMENT (continued)

considered grounds for termination of this agreement in accordance with ARS 33-1368A and loss of all deposits.

14. Security Deposit

Tenants hereby agree to pay a security deposit of $ _____ to be refunded upon vacating, return of the keys to the office and termination of this contract according to other terms herein agreed. This deposit will be held to cover any possible damage to the property. <u>No interest will be paid on this money and in no case will it be applied to back or future rent.</u> It will be held intact by Landlord until at least fourteen working days after Tenants have vacated the property. At that time Landlord will inspect the premises thoroughly and assess any damages and/or needed repairs. This deposit money <u>minus any necessary charges</u> for repairs, cleaning, etc., will then be returned to Tenant with a written explanation of deductions, within fourteen working days after they have vacated the property.

15. Cleaning Fee

Tenant hereby agrees to accept the property in its present state of cleanliness. They agree to return the property in the same condition or pay a $100. cleaning fee if Landlord has the property professionally cleaned.

16. Month-to-Month Tenancy

This is a month-to-month Rental Agreement only! It is not a lease or other long-term agreement. In accordance with Sections 33-1375 of the Arizona Statutes, after one month's rental payment has been received, this agreement may be terminated by mutual consent of the parties; or by either party giving written notice at least 30 days prior to the end of any monthly period. Any provision of this agreement may be reasonably changed by the Owner in like manner, thus THIS RENTAL CONTRACT ESTABLISHES A MONTH-TO-MONTH TENANCY ONLY! All parties agree that termination of this agreement without prior notice before _____ will constitute breach of the tenancy as agreed on Page 1, and all Security Deposits shall be forefeited in favor of the Owner as full liquidated damages at Owner's option following termination without notice.

17. Tenant Cooperation

Tenant agrees to cooperate with Owner/agent in showing property to prospective tenants, prior to termination of occupancy.

18. Removal of Landlord's Property

If anyone removes any property belonging to Landlord without the express written consent of Landlord, this will constitute abandonment and surrender of the premises by Tenant and termination by them of this Rental Agreement. Landlord may also take further legal action.

19. Tenant Insurance

No rights of storage are given by this agreement. Landlord will not be liable for any loss of Tenant's property. Tenant hereby acknowledges this and agrees to make no such claims for any losses or damages against Landlord, his agents, or employees. Tenants agree to purchase insurance—at their own expense—sufficient to protect themselves and their property from fire, theft, burglary, breakage, electrical connections. They acknowledge that if they fail to procure such insurance, it is their responsibility and they alone shall bear the consequences.

RENTAL AGREEMENT (continued)

20. Abandonment

If Tenants leave the premises unoccupied for 15 days without paying rent in advance for that month, or while owing any back rent from previous months, which has remained unpaid, the Landlord and/or his representatives have the right to take immediate possession of the property and to bar the Resident from returning. Landlord will also have the right to remove any property that the Residents have left behind and store it at Tenant's expense.

21. Lock Policy

No additional locks will be installed on any door without the written permission of Landlord. Landlord will be given duplicate keys for all locks so installed at the Tenant's expense, before they are installed.

22. Condition of Premises

The Tenants hereby acknowledge that the said property is in good condition. If there is anything about the condition of the property that is not good, they agree to report it to Landlord within 3 days of taking possession of the property. They agree that failure to file any written notice of defects will be legally binding proof that the property is in good condition at the time of occupancy.

23. Inventory and Inspection Record

An Inventory and Inspection Record has been provided for the Tenants' use. Only after this has been filled out (within the three-day time limit) will the Owner take any action to complete necessary repairs. Landlord warrants that all major systems will be functional and in good repair at time of possession. Light switches, wall plugs, doors, windows, faucets, drains, locks, toilets, sinks, heater, etc., will either be in working order or will be repaired once the Tenants have completed the Inspection and Inventory Record. Tenants are encouraged to report any necessary repairs, no matter how slight, in writing, but they are hereby advised that Landlord does not normally repair or replace nonfunctional items such as paint, carpets, etc., every time a property changes possession. Those items are scheduled for repair/replacement at regular intervals regardless of tenant turnover.

24. Tenant Responsibility

Good housekeeping is expected of everyone. Tenant agrees to keep quarters clean and in a sanitary condition. The Tenants agree not to permit any deterioration or destruction to occur while thay are occupying the property. They agree to maintain the walls, woodwork, floors, furnishings, fixtures and appliances (if any), windows, screens, doors, fences, plumbing, air-conditioning and heating, electrical and mechanical systems as well as the general structure and appearance of the property. In particular, Tenant is required to change pads on cooler in the spring, replace cooler pump when necessary, apply sealer to cooler floors, and remove all water from cooler when converting to furnace.

25. Alterations

Tenant shall make no alterations, decorations, additions or improvements in or to the premises without Landlords' prior written consent, and then only by contractors or mechanics approved by Landlord. All alterations, additions, or improvements upon the premises, made by either party, shall become the property of Landlord and shall remain upon, and be surrendered with said premises, as a part thereof, at the end of the term hereof.

RENTAL AGREEMENT (continued)

The Tenants specifically agree that no tacks, nails, screws, etc., will be driven into the walls, nor will they be marred or torn by glue or tape. They also acknowledge that they will be responsible for and pay any damage done by rain, wind, hail, tornadoes, hurricanes, etc., if this damage is caused by leaving windows open, allowing stoppage and/or overflow or water and/or sewage pipes, broken windows or doors, torn screens, broken door and window locks, etc., or any damage caused while Tenant has occupancy.

26. Maintenance of Lawns
The Tenants acknowledge that they are legally responsible for maintaining the lawns and landscaping and will be held liable for any damage caused by lack of water, abuse, or neglect.

27. Vehicle Policy
The Tenants agree never to park or store a motor home, camper, trailer, or any sort of recreational vehicle on the premises and to park only _____ automobiles, license numbers _____ only on the paved areas provided. Junk cars, cars on blocks, non-functional vehicles, or unlicensed automobiles are not permitted on property. Removal will be at the expense of the Tenant. Tenants agree that any vehicle parked on unpaved areas may be towed and stored at Tenant's expense.

28. Utilities
Resident will be responsible for payment of all utilities, garbage, water and sewer charges, telephone, gas or other bills incurred during their residency. They specifically authorize Owner to deduct amounts of unpaid bills from their Security Deposits in the event they remain unpaid after termination of this agreement.

29. Roof and Termite Alert
Tenant agrees to notify Landlord immediately if roof leaks, water spots appear on ceiling, or at the first sign of termite activity.

30. Nonliability
The Tenants hereby state that any work or repairs that need to be done will be handled by competent professionals, unless Tenants are qualified and capable of doing the work themselves and doing it properly, in a safe manner that meets all federal, state, and local regulations. Tenants further state that they will be legally responsible for any mishap they either do themselves or hire others to do. Landlord will be held free from harm and liability along with his agents and representatives. In the event that needed repairs are beyond the Tenants' capacity, they are urged to arrange for professional help.

31. Disclosure of Landlord/Agent
The Owner is _____ and may be represented at various times by his employees or agents, who will carry identification. _____ is the manager of the property and authorized to act for and on behalf of the Owner for the purpose of receiving and receipting for notices and demands and for the service of process and all other acts which Landlord could or would do if personally present. Manager's address is 1609 N. Wilmot #104C, Tucson, AZ 85712, 748-1010.

RENTAL AGREEMENT (continued)

32. Validity of Lease Provisions

Any provision set forth in this Rental Agreement which is contrary to the Arizona Residential Landlord and Tenant Act shall be treated by Landlord and Tenant as void and as if it were not set forth herein, but all other provision of the Rental Agreement shall remain in full force and effect.

33. Phone

The tenants agree to get a phone installed in the premises as soon as possible. Landlord will be given the phone number within two working days of installation and will be notified within two working days of any future changes in the phone number.

34. Access to Premises

The Owner reserves the right to enter the residence at reasonable times to inspect, make necessary repairs, supply services or show it to prospective residents, purchasers, mortgages, workmen, or contractors. Whenever practicable, a two-day notice of the Owner's intent to enter shall be given to the Resident. The Owner may also display "for rent" and "for sale" signs on the building of which the rented residence is a part.

35. Pest-Control Policy

Resident is responsible for any ongoing pest control service, if the Resident desires such a service. Owner is not responsible for any damage done to the Resident's person, or property by such pests, or to the person or property of Resident's family or any other persons on their premises.

36. Waiver

All rights given to Landlord by this agreement shall be cumulative in addition to any laws which exist or might come into being. Any exercise of any rights by Landlord or failure to exercise any rights shall not act as waiver of those or any other rights. No statement or promise by Landlord, its agents or employees, as to tenancy, repairs, amount of rent to be paid, or other terms and conditions shall be binding unless it is put in writing and made a specific part of this agreement.

37. Legal Binding

Tenant hereby states that they have the legal rights to sign for any and all other residents and to commit them to abide by this contract.

38. Terms

In this agreement the singular number where used will include the plural, the masculine gender will include the feminine, the term Owner will include Landlord, Lessor; and the term Resident will include Tenant, Lessee.

39. Full Disclosure

The Tenants signing this Rental Contract hereby state that all questions about this Rental Agreement have been answered, that they fully understand all the provisions of the agreement and the obligations and responsibilities of each party, as spelled out herein. They further state that they agree to fulfill their obligations in every respect or suffer the full legal and financial consequences of their actions or lack of action in violation of this agreement. Signature by the Tenant on this Rental Agreement is acknowledgment and he/she has received a signed copy of the Rental Agreement.

RENTAL AGREEMENT (continued)

Accepted this _____ day of _____, 19_____

_____
Owner/Agent

_____
Tenant

_____
Tenant

UTILITIES

Gas	Southwest Gas	747-3535
Electric	Tucson Electric	623-7711
Water	Tucson Water	791-3242
Trash	Tucson Collect.	791-3171
Phone	Mountain Bell	884-3300

us all the things we had to take out of our agreement and all the things we couldn't do; but when it came down to it, she had to admit that it contained nothing illegal.

Still, we were grateful for her input and we used it. We changed our contract and improved it, with her help. Now, how many people can get the services of an attorney like that for free? We figure that we got several hundred dollars' worth of legal advice before we finished going back and forth with her, and we've had no problems since.

From this we learned never to let our rental agreement out of our sight. If a tenant has too many questions about it, then he or she is not the type of tenant we want. As far as the tenants are concerned, our agreement is carved in stone. There are no compromises or changes. It is a take-it-or-leave-it proposition. Naturally, most people still have questions, but we answer them on the spot. If the prospective tenant isn't satisfied with the answer, that is the tenant's problem. We make sure each applicant understands the agreement thoroughly and completely. This is why we spend as much as an hour and a half with each prospect, and go over the agreement line by line and word by word when necessary. We gauge their responses, and then we decide whether or not they passed the interview.

We insist that the whole family—kids and all—be there when we go through this process. This is our chance to observe them closely and see how they interact with one another. Do we want these people in our house. At this point we ask ourselves, "If these people invited us for dinner, would we feel comfortable in their home? Would we feel comfortable inviting them to have dinner in our home?" If the answer is, No, we ask ourselves, "Why not?" The answer to that question often warns us that we wouldn't be comfortable renting to these people. And if we can't answer the question, we certainly take it as a warning and turn them down. This is one time we can't afford to doubt our instincts.

We never commit ourselves to rent to anyone until the interview is over and the rental contract has been signed. Here is how we go through it with prospective renters, clause by clause.

1. Rent   This establishes the official rent as $450 a month. We explain this carefully, stressing that this higher figure is the *official* rent. By letting tenants pay less than that, we are giving them a special privilege, one that can be revoked at any time. If the rent is late, a tenant loses this privilege. There is no grace period. The rent is due on time, and we hold all tenants to it. A seven-day notice is the official warning that we are ready to start eviction proceedings. We don't fool around with late payments, and we state this clearly in the rental contract right at the outset.

2. Payment of Rent   We learned this the hard way, too. People can bounce deposit checks on you, and there's nothing you can do about it. As far as the law is concerned, you haven't given them anything of value in return for the check, so you haven't lost anything.

Taking only cash (or money orders, noncancelable cashier's checks, or other certified checks) eliminates this problem. If tenants are serious, they don't mind putting up cash for the deposit and the first month's rent. If they aren't serious, this is one more good way to get rid of them. Once again, we want to make it clear to them that late payments will not be tolerated and no excuses will be accepted. Repetition is often the key to understanding.

3. Discount Program   This is the positive side. We want to emphasize the special benefit that prospective tenants will get by renting from us. We also want to reemphasize the responsibility they must bear in return.

4. Appliance(s)   Appliances are the biggest problems we have had over the years. People break them and expect us to fix them. We let them know that we aren't that kind of landlord anymore. It's spelled out in plain English so that they can't complain later that they didn't understand what they were signing.

5. Rental Collection Charge   We deliberately put the late charge in a separate clause. We want to emphasize to the tenants that late payments will cost them dearly. By putting this in a separate clause, we make it clear that late payers must pay the 5 percent late fee in addition to losing the $50 discount.

6. Bad-Check Charge   The bad-check charge is obvious. No one but an obvious professional deadbeat would dare object to this one.

7. Use   This is a very important clause. It ensures that our houses will not be used as crash pads. Also, we never run into eviction problems where strangers living in the property claim that they're legal tenants.

Legitimate tenants will ask questions when they reach this clause. Most people occasionally want friends or relatives to stay for a few days. In fact, we worry if people don't ask questions about this. That could mean that they're rule breakers who intend to do just what they want, no matter what the rental contract says.

8. Pets   This is just another way of maintaining control over the property and the tenants. Besides, it's a nuisance to have stray animals hanging around the property.

9. Nonassignment of Rental Agreement   Subleasing is dangerous for the landlord unless he maintains strict controls. We aren't going to be any more lax about subleasing than we are about picking the original tenants. It's our property, and we must approve anyone who lives there.

10. Legal Obligations   This one is another shock treatment. It's one more reminder of what happens if tenants don't pay their rent on time or live up to their other obligations.

11. Attorney's Costs   This is a bit more of the same. You can never make things too clear.

12. Repair Policy   This just restates the fact that our tenants are pretty much on their own. People who need their hands held had better rent from someone else.

13. Arizona Statutes   This lets tenants know that we have the law on our side, know all our rights under the law, and will not tolerate people who trash our properties. Spelling out the tenants' legal obligations in detail shows that we're serious. This way, tenants know what is expected of them and what won't be tolerated.

14. Security Deposit   Many landlords make the mistake of allowing tenants to apply their security deposit toward their last month's rent when they're ready to move out. This is strictly against our policy, and we spell that out clearly.

15. Cleaning Fee   This lets the tenant know that they will pay if they leave a house dirty.

16. Month-to-Month Tenancy   We don't give anyone a lease. In most states residential leases benefit only the tenants, not the landlord. You can't hold a tenant against his will for very long, and a smart landlord doesn't really want to.

17. Tenant Cooperation   Why should we lose rent every time a tenant decides to move? It's much easier to show the place before they leave.

18. Removal of Landlord's Property   This one is pretty clear. We don't let anyone steal from us. Period.

19. Tenant Insurance   This clause is necessary to cut our liability. We don't want to be responsible for our tenants' property, and this ensures that we won't be.

20. Abandonment   The last thing we need is to have a vacant property and not be able to get in and take possession until we go through an eviction. This clause saves us from getting into that sort of position.

21. Lock Policy   This ensures that we always have access to our own property.

22. Condition of Premises and *23. Inventory and Inspection Record*   This one piece of paper can sometimes tell us more about our new tenants than anything else. How many faults do they find? What sort of complaint are they making?

Of course, we are also protecting ourselves. We don't want people moving in and making demands. We also don't want them to stay a while, damage our property, and then claim that the damage was already there when they moved in. (This is the same form as the interior checklist on pages 58–60.)

24. Tenant Responsibility   This is another clause that lets people know what types of tenants we want and what duties they must perform. As usual, everything is spelled out in detail.

25. Alterations   We try to be flexible and give our tenants a lot of slack. Henry Ford once said, "They can have any color they like, as long as it's black." That's our type of flexibility.

26. Maintenance of Lawns   Clean lawns lead to clean minds and clean houses.

27. Vehicle Policy   We rent houses, not industrial property. If we wanted junkyards, we'd buy them.

28. Utilities   The tenant is living in the house and using the utilities. Why should we pay the bills?

29. Roof and Termite Alert   This makes resident managers out of tenants. They're in the property day after day. They know what's going on long before we do. It only makes sense to have them report any serious problems to us. We maintain our properties to protect our equities.

30. Nonliability   We aren't going to have contractors or subcontractors putting mechanics' liens on our properties because the tenants don't pay their bills. Nor are we going to have anyone doing inferior work on our properties and messing them up.

31. Disclosure of Landlord/Agent   This clause is required by law to protect ourselves and our agents.

32. Validity of Lease Provisions   This clause is necessary to protect us in case any part of our rental agreement is illegal, or in case it's affected by some future changes in the landlord-tenant law. If one or more provisions of our rental contract are invalid, we don't have to change the whole thing.

33. Phone   We need to be able to get in touch with our tenants promptly in case they don't pay their rent on time.

34. Access to Premises   This is part of our tenant control program. We get frequent reports on our property and the way tenants keep it.

35. Pest Control Policy   We don't rent houses with rats or roaches. If the tenants allow these pests to move in, the tenants can pay to get rid of them.

36. Waiver   This establishes that we are demanding rights for ourselves above and beyond the minimum rights granted to all landlords by state law. If prospective tenants don't like this idea, there are plenty of other landlords they can rent from.

37. Legal Binding   What sense does it make to sign a contract with someone if that contract is not legally binding on all the people it's supposed to cover?

38. Terms   This ensures that all terms used are understood. No one can weasel out on the grounds that the contract wording did not specifically include them.

39. Full Disclosure   Required by law. Tenants must be given a copy of anything they sign and be able to understand it. This clause is one more bit of protection against future lawsuits.

AN OUNCE OF PREVENTION

Some people might think that a thirty-nine-point rental agreement is a little excessive, but we find it saves us a lot of trouble. It isn't just the rental contract itself that protects us. The time we spend going over the contract is important. If people start questioning or objecting to too many items in the rental contract, we don't want them as tenants. If they can't control their children during the rental interview, what will those children do to our house?

The rental interview also gives us a chance to show good prospects our good side. Once we've scared people by warning them about what happens if they're bad tenants, we also tell them what happens if they're good ones. They can get a handyman for a day to do all their maintenance chores. They can move up from one of our cheaper houses to one of our nicer ones as their family grows. They can even buy a house from us on good terms when they're tired of renting. We use the stick, but we also use the carrot. We want our tenants to be good because they want to be good, not just because they're afraid of us.

Most tenants want to know that there are definite rules that will be enforced. It gives them limits, and a sense of stability. That's how they know that you care. Sometimes they deliberately misbehave just to get your attention. The rental interview is the time to let them know that you won't tolerate that sort of behavior. Good tenants will be glad to know that they can go just so far and no further.

Does that last paragraph sound familiar? If you've ever heard or read anything about training an animal, or raising a child, it probably does. It's not that we think all tenants are animals, or childlike. But we've found through experience that these same techniques work in every situation where a few people have to establish control over a number of others. For instance, business owners and office supervisors have to manage their workers. Did you see the movie *An Officer and a Gentleman* or an older film called *The G.I.?* Those were both excellent stories that illustrated how military organizations establish authority so that new recruits can be trained in the skills they'll need in life-or-death emergencies.

You and your tenants probably won't be called on to repel an enemy invasion, so you don't need to train renters as thoroughly as you would if you were running a boot camp. But you are involved in a business together, one that's important to your present and future welfare. In order for that business to run smoothly and to be as pleasant and profitable as possible for you, the landlord, you have to train your tenants in their roles. Once they know what's expected of them, and how firmly you require them to follow your rules, you'll all be happier.

The rental interview and the rental agreement are the initial steps in this training course, and they'll get you off to a good start. For some tenants, this will be all the training they'll ever need. Others, however, will try to test you. They think you should make exceptions for them, or they want to see if you really mean to hold them to all those clauses in your agreement.

You have to respond to these tests firmly and immediately. If your new busboy, factory apprentice, or secretary started taking an extra half-hour for lunch the second week on the job, you'd stop it the first time it happened. Otherwise, you'd soon have an employee who comes in late, leaves early, and calls in sick five times a month. If your teenager takes your car without asking, you make it clear that if anyone walks everywhere for the next five years, it's not going to be Mom or Dad. And if the new puppy makes puddles on the rug . . .

Well, the person in charge has to do the training. As a landlord, you're in charge and you have to make that clear from the start. On the next few pages we'll show you some more of our tenant forms, which should be self-explanatory, and then we'll devote an entire chapter to tips on handling those hard-to-train tenants.

**(If tenants can't come up with
cash for their deposit, we'll
take valuables instead.)**

ASSETS IN LIEU OF SECURITY DEPOSITS

In consideration for $340.00 security deposit, Mr. and Mrs.
_____(prospective tenant)_____ have provided Irene V.
Milin, Manager of 2560 S. Kevin, Tucson, AZ with title to
their 1983 GMC Pickup, serial #TCL148F732138.

At such time as Mr. and Mrs. ____(prospective tenant)____
present Irene Milin with $340.00 (three hundred and forty
dollars) in cash, this title will be immediately released.

_____   _____

Irene V. Milin/Agent   Date

I,____(prospective tenant)____ have agreed and understand
the above contract. I have authorized Irene V. Milin to
hold my title to my 1983 GMC Pickup, serial number
#TCL148F732138, until such time as I remit $340.00 (three
hundred and forty dollars) in cash to cover security
deposit for 2560 S. Kevin, Tucson, AZ.

_____   _____

Tenant   Date

CONSENT FOR MAINTAINING A PET

This memorandum constitutes a representation by the tenant and a consent by the landlord for maintenance in house at _____ (address) _____, of the following described pet:

> The animal is a _____.
> The breed is _____.
> The weight is not more than _____ pounds.
> The height is not more than _____ inches.
> The color is _____.
> Its name is _____.

This consent is given as a condition of or part of a lease/rental agreement dated _____ relative to the house named and renewals thereof. The sum of $_____ per month will be added to the basic rent by the landlord as a pet fee and is not refundable, but is a charge in addition to the rent payable under the lease.

It is expressly provided that the following rules are to be observed by the tenant if the pet is a dog:

> It shall at all times be kept on leash when outside the house.

The tenant is to be fully responsible for any damage to property of owner or of others which may result from the maintenance of the pet.

Landlord reserves the right to revoke this consent on three days' notice to tenant, if in the opinion of landlord's employees, the pet has been a nuisance to other tenants or has not been maintained according to these rules. In the event consent is revoked, tenant agrees to forthwith discontinue maintenance of the pet, and failure to so discontinue shall be a breach of the lease.

Signed this _____ day of _____, 19_____.

_____
Tenant

_____
Landlord

TENANT DISCLAIMER LETTER

_____

Address

_____

Date

To Whom It May Concern:

_____(tenant's name)_____, hereafter known as the
tenant(s), hereby states and guarantees that all work performed
by himself/herself/themselves and any agents, employees, or independent contractors and subcontractors he/she/they may retain,
shall be done only with the proper permits from all relevant
state, local, or federal agencies and shall conform to all
state, local, and federal building codes. Tenant(s) further
state(s) that all work shall be done at his/her/their own expense and risk. The tenant(s) shall bear all liability for any
charges for labor, materials, fees, legal charges.
   The owner of the property at _____(address)_____
shall have absolutely no responsibility or liability for any
materials, labor, legal fees, or any other costs or fees. No
expense shall be incurred by tenant(s) _____(name)_____
which could result in a lien being placed against the property
or any claim or legal action made against the owner _____
___(name)_____ or any managers or representatives of the
owner. In the event of any legal action, _____(name)_____,
the tenant(s) shall bear full responsibility for the owner's
_____(name)_____ entire costs and legal fees. The
tenant(s) _____(name)_____ and not the owner
_____(name)_____ shall be fully responsible and
liable for all mishaps or accidents and/or any claims arising
therefrom, although any improvements become the property of the
owner.

_____   _____

Tenant   Date

_____   _____

Tenant   Date

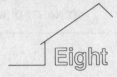

Eight

Training Tenants to Obey Your Rules

If it costs them money each and every time they misbehave, then tenants will quickly learn to follow the rules. You can't let them off with a warning and tell them that next time they'll be penalized. You have to punish them right away, the first time they get out of line. This may sound harsh, or even cruel, but tenants don't respond to threats and promises. They do respond to immediate rewards and punishments.

If they break your rules, you have to respond at once. Don't wait for the second or third time. If their rent is due and you haven't received it, call them. That's why you want their phone numbers. Threaten them with a loss of privileges. Remind them that the rent is due. Tell them how you'd hate to see them lose their discount. If they don't come in by the second of the month and bring you the rent, post a seven-day notice on their door. This is a legal notice that you're starting eviction proceedings.

If you don't have their rent by the fifth of the month, send them a Mailgram. This is just like a telegram, but it's cheaper. You buy it at the post office, and it's delivered to the tenant in person. Send it to the company where the tenant works. Legally, it must be addressed "Private and Confidential." But this way, his bosses and co-workers will all know he received it. Everyone will wonder what it's all about, and they'll pester him with embarassing questions.

Would you want your bosses and co-workers to know that you didn't pay your rent? This is likely to have more effect than sending the Mailgram to the tenant at home, where he can read it in privacy. You want the world to know that Demanding Daniel is a deadbeat. If it weren't for the cost, you'd take out billboards and TV spots to advertise the news. Once Daniel realizes this, he will usually pay up. If he doesn't, then get thee to a lawyer and have him thrown out.

If you let the tenants develop bad habits, you're in trouble. Once they get used to paying the rent late, they start thinking about what else can they get away with. Pretty soon they won't pay their rent at all.

Stay on top of your tenants at the beginning, and you can ease up later. Just punishing them for paying the rent late isn't enough. You also have to keep an eye on them until you're sure that they're taking proper care of your property.

SETTING UP A SURVEILLANCE NETWORK

Develop a spy network. Make sure at least one of the neighbors has your phone number. You want to know right away if the lawn isn't being cut or too many cars are being parked on the property, or the dogs are running loose. The neighbors want to keep the neighborhood up, and so do you. If the tenant doesn't cooperate, he's going to have everybody coming down on him at once.

Your property will appreciate the way it should only if you maintain it properly. The tenant is there in the property every day; you are not. You need the tenants' help. Make it clear to the tenant that the discount is directly tied to that cooperation. If he breaks the rules, he loses it, even if he has paid his rent on time. Once the tenant realizes this and realizes that you know how he's keeping the house, he'll usually do his job. If he thinks that you don't really care, he'll goof off. You get back whatever you put into training your tenants. If you're lax and/or inconsistent, you'll pay the price later.

You can turn your tenant surveillance program into a positive thing by enlisting your handyman as part of your spy team. As a conscientious landlord, you want to send the handyman to inspect all your properties every six months or so. That is both good maintenance policy and good landlord-tenant relations. The tenants should appreciate the fact that you care so much about the house they're living in. Naturally, while your handyman is there, he'll be looking and observing, and then he'll come back and report to you. Is the place clean and neat? Are the tenants changing the filters in the heater and/or the air conditioner the way they're supposed to? Have they chipped any paint or allowed the kids to write on the walls?

You may feel uncomfortable about using these tactics at first, but they'll help you protect your assets. Have you ever tried to rent a car? You need a major credit card and references, and the rental company wants to know your home address, your local address, and how long you intend to keep the car. You either take out extra insurance, or you pay for the first couple of hundred dollars in damages. Car rental companies don't take any chances with their cars. What's a rental car worth? Six thousand dollars to ten thousand dollars? What's the average rental house worth? A lot more than that. Shouldn't you be at least as careful as the car rental companies? You're turning a valuable piece of property over to virtual strangers and you'd better take precautions to safeguard your investment.

MAKING TENANTS FEEL AT HOME

Besides developing a spy network and being prepared to take punitive measures against rule breakers, you have to use positive motivation. You have to give your new tenants a sense of belonging. You have to give them the feeling that your house is their home, a place where they will live for a long time, not just a temporary resting place.

People don't care about your house unless they feel they have a stake in the property. If they're planning to move in a short time, why should they put any effort into the house? We want tenants who will improve our houses and leave them better than they find them, and in order to get them, we go out of our way to set up the proper atmosphere.

When tenants are ready to move into one of our houses, our office manager gives them a list of the schools in the area, the phone numbers for the police and fire departments, and any other relevant information, such as the phone number for the gas and electric company, the water company, and so on. They also get a written sheet with our office number and the hours we're open. They're given another number to call only in case of emergencies. We don't want to be bothered about petty problems, but we don't want to be unaware of serious problems, either. A sample of this information sheet is on the next page.

Making tenants pay for certain things themselves also helps give them a sense of responsibility and makes them feel as though the house is really theirs. We encourage our handyman to get involved in this by selling things like filters for the heater and cooler. When he comes around to make his inspections, he sells the tenants what they need to maintain our house. This is good for us, and it's good for the tenants, because it makes it easy and convenient for them to live up to the rental agreement. It's also good for the handyman, since he makes extra money and it encourages him to take an active part in our tenant management program. This, in turn, makes the tenants feel better, because they feel that the handyman, too, is taking a personal interest in them.

RAISING THE RENTS

Once the tenants are properly housebroken and under control, it's time to start thinking about the income from the property. How soon and how much can you raise the rent? Every situation is different. It depends largely on the local rental market. What is fair-market rent for the area? If your rent is low, then raise it right away. If the rent is close to fair-market value, you'll have to wait a while—six months to a year—before you raise it. Obviously, your decision will also depend on how you feel about the tenant.

If he has responded well to your basic training program, you don't want to drive him away. You want him to stay a while and keep your property stable. This can be more important than squeezing out a few extra dollars in rent. If you do raise the rent, you want to do it tactfully. We have a special letter we

COMMUNITY INFORMATION

Property Address:_____

School Info
  Elementary:
    Name:_____
    Address:_____
    Phone:_____
  Junior High:
    Name:_____
    Address:_____
    Phone:_____
  High:
    Name:_____
    Address:_____
    Phone:_____

Utilities
Water	791-3242
Gas	747-3535
Elec	623-7711
Sewer	326-4333
Trash	791-3171
Phone	884-3300
Cable	623-2255
HBO	881-1223

Public Services
Police	911
Fire	911
Medical	911
Crime	911
Bus	882-9613

send out in situations like this (see page 149). It apologizes for raising the rent and goes on to explain why we had to do it even though we really didn't want to.

Timing is probably at least as important as tact and courtesy when you want to raise a good tenant's rent. We always try to wait until the kids are in school and the family is all settled in before we hit them with any rent raises. February is our favorite month. People are settled down, and they're usually broke from the holidays, so they're probably less likely to move then than at any other time of the year.

If our tenants do move, they have to give us notice, and they have to let us show the house while they're still living in it. We don't lose rent for anybody if we can help it. As it's turned out, many of our tenants don't really understand what the notice requirement means, so they often wind up paying our advertising costs before they leave.

State law says that tenants have to give us thirty days' notice before the end of the rental period if they want to move. This means they have to give us notice by the thirty-first of the month, but most of them wait until the first, the start of an entirely new rental period. When they do this, we inform them that they are too late and will have to wait until the end of the month to give us notice. This means they have to stay an extra month—unless they want to pay the advertising costs. In that case, we will let them go as soon as we find a new tenant.

If they refuse, that's fine. We simply won't do any advertising at our expense until thirty days have gone by. It's such an effective way to prevent vacancies that we almost never have a vacancy problem. That's in line with our entire management philosophy: Whenever possible, we put all the burden and responsibility on the tenants.

REWARD THE GOOD TENANTS

We reward good tenants for being loyal and doing their jobs. When they've been with us for a year, we celebrate their anniversary. We give them the services of our handyman for an entire day. He'll make repairs or improvements on the house, or do their personal maintenance chores.

We'll even give exceptionally good tenants a lease option if they think they might want to buy one of our houses. But no one gets a break on the rent. That stays at least at the level it was set at when the tenant moved in. It can go higher, but never lower.

If our tenants want to improve our houses by adding things like decks or fences, that's great. It raises the value of our property, and it means the tenant is less likely to leave at any time in the near future. All this is nice, but it doesn't mean that we're going to lower the rent, or even pay for the materials. We don't want any possible liability for any work our tenants might do to our houses. That wouldn't be good business.

One large landlord we know actually charges his tenants for the improvements they make. He sends out a form letter that thanks them for taking such good care of his property, and then informs them that all their beautiful work has caused his property taxes to go up. Therefore, he has no choice; he has to raise their rent. But since he's so nice, and they're such good tenants, he tells them he'll split the increase with them. If his taxes have supposedly gone up $20 a month, he raises their rent by only $10 a month.

THE RENT BELONGS TO THE LANDLORD

We aren't that grasping. We raise tenants' rents only at the next scheduled interval, not immediately after they make improvements. This way, the tenants understand that it's their house, and any improvements they make are only to make themselves more comfortable. They may get other rewards, such as being allowed to buy the house from us, but they won't get any breaks on the rent.

The late Charles Hughes, of High Point, North Carolina, one of the wealthiest and most successful landlords we ever met, once summed up the landlord's dilemma quite simply. "Most people can't manage rental property" he said, "because they are afraid to say, 'I want my money.' "

We've never been afraid to say, "I want my money." If we don't get it, things start to happen fast—faster than most deadbeats are prepared for, even if they're pros. First of all, we have the security deposit. Our contract states that none of it will be credited toward rent. The day a tenant is late in paying the rent, we file to evict him. But if we have to evict him, at least we have the security deposit, and we keep it. Then we get a judgment against him for the rent he owes in addition.

If a tenant bounces a check on us, that's it. After that, it's strictly money orders or cash. Whenever possible, we get our tenants to open accounts at our bank. That way, we can just have the money automatically transferred from their account to ours each month. (We also get points with the bank for bringing in new customers.)

On the other hand, our tenants know that we uphold our end as landlords. We'll do whatever we're supposed to do and whatever we say we're going to do. Being a landlord is a two-way street. If we don't take care of our responsibilities, how can we expect the tenants to meet theirs? Once the tenants realize that they can trust us to do exactly what we say, they usually pay their rent regularly and on time with no problem. If they don't, then we move on to the next chapter and get rid of them.

We garnishee wages if we have to, and slap judgments on people, and ruin their credit ratings. We want our money and we intend to get it, preferably with a minimum of fuss. But occasionally, all our systems break down. Even with our tough screening procedures and our careful training techniques after a tenant is in the house, occasionally a deadbeat slips through. Then we have to get rid of him . . . which takes us to our next chapter.

Nine

Getting Rid of Bad Tenants

We choose our tenants carefully, but we do occasionally make mistakes. What we don't do, however, is waste time worrying about them. If we make a mistake, we want to correct it as quickly as possible. Once we decide a tenant is undesirable, we make plans to get rid of him. If he's not paying rent, we start eviction proceedings on the day after it's due. First we send him a Mailgram as a reminder, then we put an eviction notice on the door.

If a Mailgram delivered at his workplace and a seven-day notice on his door aren't enough, then we go right to court—with the tenant picking up the bill. We make it clear in the Mailgram that the tenant will either pay up or be responsible for the legal costs. If he doesn't take this seriously, then it's his own fault.

We don't fool around trying to do evictions on our own. That's what lawyers are for. In fact, we had to fire one lawyer because he was taking too long to get us into court and that was costing us money. We found another lawyer who specializes in evictions, and he cut down the time it took to get into court from almost six weeks to two. This not only saves us money but it has a devastating psychological effect on tenants. Once they realize they can't play games with us, their attitude improves markedly. It's one thing to figure that you can stall off eviction for a month and a half. It's another thing to know that you'll be out within four weeks.

Generally, though, we try *not* to go to court. Most tenants respond well to the Mailgram reminding them they're late with the rent and then if necessary the seven-day notice of eviction. Samples of these follow.

We're lucky in Arizona. The state laws are good, and we can get nonpaying tenants out quickly. In California, where we also own property, it's a different story. There, the laws are tenant-oriented, and it can take months to get a tenant out if he wants to fight you. The first thing to do is find out what the laws are in your area, so that you know what you're up against.

ALTERNATIVES TO EVICTION

Before we get involved in an eviction, we always try to examine all the alternatives and keep our losses to a minimum. Any time you have to go to court to force a tenant out, you're probably going to lose money.

When a hostile tenant occupies the house, you can't show it. This means you are going to lose rent because you can't begin to select your new tenant until you get the current one out. There'll be a lag time of anywhere from a week to a month or more before you can get the new tenant into your house.

Paying Bad Tenants to Leave

Sometimes the best idea is just to pay the old tenants to leave without a fight. Swallow your pride, give them part of their security deposit back, and make a clean, fresh start. If you're lucky, there won't be any real damage to your property. If all you have to do is paint and/or clean and straighten the place up a little bit, consider yourself fortunate. Get the work done as quickly as possible and get the house back on the market. Then you can worry about going after your previous tenant.

Your first priority is always to get your money. Being a landlord is a business, and like any other business, it runs on money —you have to keep it coming in faster than it's going out. Getting revenge on a tenant is secondary. Get your money first, and worry about the rest later.

MAILGRAM

MIDDLETOWN, VA. 22645

A-0628563075002 03/16/82 ICS IPHRNCZ CSP PHXB
1 6027481010 MGM TDRN TUCSON AZ 03-16 1043P EST

MICHAEL J. MILIN
5055 EAST BROADWAY C214
TUCSON AZ 85711

THIS MAILGRAM IS A CONFIRMATION COPY OF THE FOLLOWING MESSAGE:

 6027481010 MGM TDRN TUCSON AZ 54 03-16 1043P EST

542 WEST INEZ
TUCSON AZ 85705

HAVE NOT RECEIVED MARCH RENT. IF RENT IS NOT REMITTED BEFORE 500PM
THURSDAY MARCH 18, EVICTION PROCEEDINGS WILL BEGIN AND YOU WILL BE
CHARGED AN ADDITIONAL $137.00 FOR ATTORNEY FEES. CONTACT ME
IMMEDIATELY REGARDING THIS SITUATION.

MICHAEL J MILIN

22:45 EST

MGMCOMP

ARIZONA 7-DAY LETTER

_____
Date

Dear _____(tenant)_____,

The monthly payment on the residence at _____(address)_____
was due on _____(due date)_____. The regular payment of
$_____ plus $_____ late charge, for a total of $_____,
is now overdue. Please remit this amount immediately.

If we have not received payment within 8 days, it is our intention to terminate the rental agreement/lease, and we require
that the premises be vacated immediately.

Such requirement is per ARIZONA REVISED STATUTES, TITLE 33,
CHAPTER 10, ARIZONA RESIDENTIAL LANDLORD AND TENANT ACT, SECTION
33-1368.

33-1368   Noncompliance with Rental Agreement by Tenant
                      Failure to Pay Rent

A. Except as provided in this chapter, if there is a material
noncompliance by the tenant with the rental agreement, the landlord may deliver a written notice to the tenant specifying the
acts and omissions constituting the breach and that the rental
agreement will terminate upon a date not less than thirty days
after receipt of the notice if the breach is not remedied in
fourteen days. If there is a noncompliance by the tenant with
Section 33-1341 materially affecting health and safety, the
landlord may deliver a written notice to the tenant specifying
the acts and omissions constituting the breach and that the
rental agreement will terminate upon a date not less than twenty
days after receipt of the notice if the breach is not remedied
in ten days. However, if the breach is remediable by repair or
the payment of damages or otherwise, and the tenant adequately
remedies the breach prior to the date specified in the notice,
the rental agreement will not terminate.

B. If rent is unpaid when due and the tenant fails to pay rent
within seven days after written notice by the landlord of
nonpayment and his intention to terminate the rental agreement
if the rent is not paid within that period of time, the landlord
may terminate the rental agreement. Prior to judgment in an
action brought by landlord under this subsection, the tenant may
have the rental agreement reinstated by tendering the past due
but unpaid periodic rent, reasonable attorneys fees incurred by
the landlord and court costs, if any.

C. Except as provided in this chapter, the landlord may
recover damages, obtain injunctive relief or recover possession
of the premises pursuant to an action in forcible detainer for
any noncompliance by the tenant with the rental agreement or
Section 33-1341.

D. The remedy provided in Subsection C is in addition to any
right of the landlord arising under Subsection A.

Very truly yours,

If a tenant damages your property and/or sticks you for rent, there are several things you can do. If he has a job, you can attach his wages. You can ruin his credit and see to it that he never borrows again. But isn't it easier to prevent the tenant from costing you money in the first place? You have to keep your head. Don't let landlording become a game of retaliation and revenge.

We keep a close watch on our tenants. We try not to let things get to the point where we have to evict anyone. If a tenant is late paying the rent on a regular basis, or is quarrelsome, or is lazy about maintaining the property, we raise his rent. You'll see the polite, apologetic letter we send to good tenants when we raise their rent in the next chapter. But our bad tenants get a very different letter.

When we want someone out, we pull no punches. There are no apologies, no excuses: just a simple demand for more money. There is also no mention of the 10 percent yearly rent increase. The increase is usually $50 to $100 the very next month, depending on how badly we want to get rid of the tenant. Usually they leave. If the tenant pays it, then it's worth putting up with him, since we'll be getting between $25 and $75 a month above normal market rent for the area.

If the tenant pays his rent late, we'll also get an extra $50 a month, because the tenant will lose his discount. At that point, he'll be paying between $75 and $125 above the normal market rent. If he pays at least five days late, we collect a late fee, too. It all adds up.

If the tenant decides not to pay the increases, it's his choice. If he doesn't want to pay, he moves. That saves us the trouble of evicting him. We don't deliberately look for confrontations with tenants. In fact, we do all we can to avoid them. Following is the letter we send to the tenants we don't like.

We Play for Keeps

If tenants who receive our sudden rent increase try to contest it and then refuse to either pay the increase or move, we inform them that they have violated the rental contract. They can either agree to renegotiate the higher rent, or they can be evicted. The

SAMPLE RENT INCREASE LETTER FOR BAD TENANTS

_____
Date

Dear Mr. and Mrs. Tenant:

Death, taxes, rent increases. These are unpleasant facts of life that none of us can avoid. Our accountant tells us we are in trouble. Our expenses are going up. The taxes have increased, the insurance premiums have increased, and our maintenance costs have gone through the roof. The only thing that hasn't gone up is our income.

No business can run that way, and ours is no exception. If we go out of business, the bank will take away the house and you will lose your home. None of us wants that, so our only alternative is to pass some of our increased costs on to you.

Naturally we are not just going to spring this on you without warning, so your rent for this month will remain the same. Starting next month, however, it will increase to $_____. However, you will of course continue to receive our good tenant discount of $50.00 a month, so you will pay only $_____.

Enclosed is a new rental agreement. Please initial each page, sign the final page, and send it back to us as soon as possible. If this puts an impossible strain on your budget and you decide to move, let us know immediately. We must have the signed rental agreement back by _____(date)_____.

Sincerely,

Michael J. Milin

choice is theirs. At that point, some of them agree to pay more money, but usually they move out. If they don't, they pay all the legal costs for their own eviction. Which would you do if you were in that spot?

One nice little touch we've added to the eviction process is to have the seven-day notice delivered by a policeman in uniform. That seems to shake people up. They don't like the idea. The fact that the policeman is off duty doesn't seem to matter very much. Most people get fairly upset when they see that uniform.

If that doesn't work and the tenants still won't leave or pay the rent, we'll have the sheriff—the real, on-duty sheriff—throw them out after we've gone to court and gotten an order for eviction. With about one hundred houses, we have never had to send out the sheriff yet. But if we ever have to, we won't hesitate. We'll do it, even though we know it can be brutal. In our county, the sheriff doesn't play around. If tenants refuse to leave peacefully, the deputies will subdue them and handcuff them to the nearest tree. The neighbors always peek out to watch, and it's a terrible experience for the evicted tenants. But it's also terrible to use someone's property without fair payment.

We view tenants living in one of our houses without paying a fair rent as stealing from us. We worked hard to learn everything we know about real estate, and then to buy and manage all our properties. We still have to make payments to the bank, whether we receive our rent or not. We also have to pay our management and maintenance staff. If we let a few tenants have a free ride for very long, we'd lose too much money. Eventually we might have to sell our properties and lay off the people who work for us.

This wouldn't be fair to anyone. Most of our tenants rent because they can't afford to buy, so if we had to sell our houses, all the good people who pay their rent and take care of our properties would lose their homes. Some of them have been living in those houses for years; they have friends on the block, gardens and flowers they've carefully nurtured, rooms they've decorated to please themselves, and close ties to the community. Their children have playmates in the neighborhood and at the local schools. These kids have their favorite teachers, belong to scout troops and clubs, and know all the best places to play. Why should these families be forced to pull up their roots and find new homes just because a few selfish, irresponsible people don't pay rent?

As for the people who work for us, they enjoy their jobs, but not enough to keep on working for us if we couldn't pay their salaries. They're all nice, conscientious people who pay their bills and take care of their families, so if we let our finances slide, those people would be out looking for new jobs. They're all bright and good workers, so it wouldn't take any of them long to find new positions; but it's never fun to be out on the street wondering where your next paycheck will come from.

And yes, of course, we have selfish motives, too. After all, we're human. We know that if we had to, we could start with nothing again tomorrow, and be right back where we are today in two or three years. But why should we do that if we don't have to? And if we pay attention to our business, and to our cash flow, we shouldn't have to.

That is why the very day we begin to have doubts about a tenant, we take a tough stance. We're responsible for our own business, for our work and our life-style, and the well-being of our family, our employees, and our good tenants. We accept that responsibility, and we even enjoy it, so we'll do whatever is necessary to live up to it. We refuse to put hundreds of people through the upheaval that could result if we didn't see to it that all our tenants live up to the agreements they sign.

That's why we're so careful about our choice of tenants and why when an occasional mistake slips through we go all out to correct that mistake. We do everything we can to get that tenant out of our property and then to make sure we get all the money that's coming to us.

The most important thing is to get a judgment against a bad tenant. This is how we get our money. Once the judgment is filed and recorded, it follows the dishonest tenant like a shadow. He can't get a job, a loan, or a credit card without having to explain why our judgment is on his record. If he goes to rent another house or an apartment, and the landlord does a credit check, our nonpaying tenant is through before he even gets started. Before his boss gives him his paycheck, money will be taken out for us. Like the IRS, we get our money before he gets his. If he has a bank account, we can attach that, too. Sooner or later, he will have to deal with us to clear his name. Since we have his social security number and the number of his driver's license and the license on his car, it isn't too hard for us to track him down. The only way he can really escape is to move out of the area.

If he does that, we just say good riddance, and go on to other things. Some losses are unavoidable in any business. We just try to keep ours to a minimum and concentrate our efforts on the subject for our next chapter, "Keeping the Good Tenants."

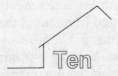

Ten

Keeping the Good Tenants

Before you can worry about keeping the good tenants, you have to get the bad ones out. Otherwise, the good ones will never stay. Therefore, on the following pages, we have some more forms for you. First and most important is the "Acceptance of Partial Payment and Nonwaiver Agreement." If a tenant is not paying his rent, we want to get at least part of what he owes us if we can. Most tenants are willing and able to pay at least part of the rent, even if they have lost their jobs, but we couldn't accept the money if we didn't get them to sign this form.

This form states clearly that we are not waiving any of our rights under the eviction statutes of our state just because we are accepting partial payment. If the tenant acknowledges that he owes us the entire amount due, not just what he is paying, his partial payment does not stop the eviction. And if he doesn't come up with the rest of the money before the eviction date set by the court, he will be out in the street.

Next is the "Security Deposit Refund Sheet." Assuming the tenant moves out voluntarily and we are not required to evict him, this form gives a breakdown of what portion of his security deposit we have kept (if any) and why. This way, there are no arguments or recriminations later.

Then we have the "Tenant Move-Out Sheet," for our records, so we know the history of each of our houses and each of our tenants right up until they leave us. Finally there's the

"Hold Harmless Agreement for Moving Tenant" to protect us from false and frivolous claims.

As anxious as we are to get rid of troublemakers, we don't forget about keeping our good tenants. In fact, that's the real heart and soul of our management system. Turnover reduces profit and so we do everything we can to reduce turnover.

Once a tenant has proven himself by taking care of the property and paying his rent on time, we want to be sure we don't lose him. He's a valuable asset. No company can run for very long without good employees, so we do all we can to promote loyalty. You might say we use the Japanese system of management. We want our "employees" to feel as though they have a stake in the company. We want them to feel that they are part of a family that will take care of them, as long as they obey the rules. And it's true. We look after and respect our good tenants.

Once they're on our good-tenant list, people can send us referrals. Their friends and relatives can apply to rent houses from us. Good tenants can also move up from one house to a better one as their family and/or their income grows. They also continue to enjoy below-market rent. This is one of the keys to our program. We set our rents about $25 below market (counting the $50 discount) and then try not to raise them for the good tenants. We lose a little income this way, but we gain stability. Our tenants stay a long time, and they don't give us any trouble.

GOOD TENANTS BECOME BUYERS

About the only trouble we have with our good tenants is that they move out when they buy homes. The people who make good, responsible tenants don't want to be renters forever; they want to own their own home. Now that interest rates are down, this is becoming a problem. Before, our tenants couldn't afford to buy, but now a lot of them can. We do all we can to discourage them. We even give out a pamphlet listing all the advantages of renting and all the costs of ownership.

ACCEPTANCE OF PARTIAL PAYMENT
AND NONWAIVER AGREEMENT

Date: _____

Owner: _____

Tenant: _____

Address: _____

I/we the undersigned, acknowledge that my/our rent was due and payable on the _____ day of _____, 19_____. In accordance with my/our Rental Agreement, I/we understand this constituted a breach, and could cause termination of our occupancy and legal action by management. I/we understand that the total rent due and owing is $_____, which includes any and all unpaid rent and any properly assessed late charges in the amount of $_____. I/we wish to pay this amount in the following manner:

_____

_____

_____

_____

_____

_____

In accordance with Arizona Revised Statutes, Section 33-1371, I/we understand and agree that management does not waive its right under the law or under my/our Rental Agreement. I/we reaffirm my/our agreement to pay rent not later than the _____ day of each month and understand and agree that failure to pay any of the amounts stated above by the dates so specified shall cause all of said amounts to become immediately due and payable in full and also entitle management to immediately commence legal proceedings, through forcible detainer action, without further demand of notice.

_____

Resident

_____

Resident

Received this _____ day of _____, 19_____.

By: _____, Manager

SECURITY DEPOSIT REFUND SHEET

Tenant Name _____

Property Address _____

Move-out Date _____

Security Deposit Taken: $ _____

Deductions:
   1. Cleaning   _____
   2. Weeds   _____
   3. Locks   _____
   4. Rent   _____
   5. Advertising   _____
   6. Pest-infestation services _____
   7. Repairs   _____
      a. _____
      b. _____
      c. _____
   8. Utilities   _____
   9. Other   _____
  10. Other   _____

Total Deductions: $ _____
Amount Refunded $ _____

Check # _____

Forwarding Address   _____

_____

_____

TENANT MOVE-OUT SHEET

Tenant Name _____

Property Address _____

Date Moved In _____   Rent at Time of Move In _____

Date Moved Out_____   Rent at Time of Move Out_____

Date Rerented _____   Amount Rented at _____

Reason for Moving _____
_____

30-day Notice given?   [ ] Yes   [ ] No

Forwarding Address:

_____

_____

_____

Security Deposit Taken _____

Amount Refunded _____

Comments: _____
_____
_____
_____
_____
_____
_____
_____

HOLD HARMLESS AGREEMENT FOR MOVING TENANT

In consideration of moving, including labor without charge and the dropping of the evictions costs and fees, _____ (tenant) _____ do hereby hold Landlord and his agents harmless from any claims for damage incurred in said move.

_____ (tenant) _____ further releases Landlord and his agents from any and all claims as a result of tenancy.

_____   _____
Tenant   Date

_____   _____
Witnessed by   Date

LEASE OPTIONS FOR GOOD TENANTS

Of course, some of our best tenants insist on buying a house anyway, and in that case, we feel that they might as well buy from us. We'll sell a good tenant a house on a lease option, for example. This means that they pay us an option fee up front (usually about $1,000) and then go on renting from us. We give them an option to buy the house some time in the future in exchange for their $1,000. Often the option will guarantee them a fixed price, generally the current market value of the house plus about 15 percent to 20 percent.

For example, let's say we have a house that's worth $60,000 at current market value. If we have a good tenant living there who is interested in buying it, we might give him a one- or two-year option to purchase the house at $69,000 or $72,000. If he decides to exercise the option, we'll give him favorable terms, such as a low down payment. If he doesn't choose to buy the house, we keep the $1,000 option fee, and more importantly, we've kept him locked in as a tenant.

It works something like this:

Property Value	$60,000
Option Price	$72,000
Option Fee	$ 1,000

Sometimes we'll even credit part of the tenant's rent toward the down payment—*if* he decides to exercise the option.

First Right of Refusal Options

With the first right of refusal option, we would set the purchase price—usually based on an appraisal by an independent fee appraiser—at the time the tenant decided to exercise the option, or when we decided that we were ready to sell. If the tenant didn't want to pay the appraisal price, or if someone else made an offer and the tenant didn't want to match it, the option would be canceled automatically.

Performance Options

If we have a very good tenant, we might even give him a performance option. This allows him to become part owner of the property just by living up to his part of the agreement for three years. For example, we have a house that rents for $350 a month, and we have a good, proven tenant living in it. We might offer him the following deal: He will pay us $450 a month, and at the end of three years, he will automatically go on title as half owner.

When we sign an agreement like this, we record it, and the title company holds two deeds. One is a grant deed signed by us, which gives the tenant a half interest in the property. The other is a quit claim deed signed by the tenant. This cancels the tenant's interest in the property. If he faithfully pays his rent on time each month, the grant deed will automatically be recorded after the thirty-sixth payment. If he is more than fifteen days late with any of his payments, the title company will automatically record the quit claim deed. This means the tenant will be just a tenant again, nothing more. He can stay in the house as long as he pays his rent, which stays at $450, but he will never be half owner.

Assuming that the tenant does live up to his half of the agreement, then at the end of three years, he will go on title as half owner of the house and he will be entitled to half the appreciation from that point forward, as well as half the tax write-off.

For example, let's say we buy a house today for $70,000 and we sign a three-year equity share option agreement with the tenant. This doesn't mean the tenant is entitled to half the appreciation over and above $70,000. His half ownership of the property doesn't start until the equity-share option period has expired at the end of three years. At that time we get the property appraised to find out the current value, and this becomes the base price for the equity-share agreement.

Let's say the property appraises for $85,000 at the end of the three-year equity share option period. This means $85,000 is the base price we will work with and the tenant is entitled to half the appreciation over and above that amount. If we decide to hold the property for another three years and then we agree to sell it for $100,000, then the tenant-co-owner would get $7,500 —half the difference between the $85,000 base price and the $100,000 sales price—and we would get the rest.

A HAPPY TENANT IS A SOLID TENANT

We also try to help our tenants in other ways, such as helping them find employment. This doesn't mean that we'll accept a new tenant who doesn't have a job, and then help him find one. But once a tenant has been in one of our houses long enough for us to know that he (or she) is reliable, we'll let him or her work on our other houses. We'll try to help our tenants find new jobs if they lose one. We aren't an employment agency, but we can often give them tips. Or sometimes we even know people who are looking to hire someone.

However, we don't believe in letting new tenants work on the houses they want to move into in lieu of rent. If people haven't got the money for a security deposit and need to work it off, they aren't the responsible type of tenant we want. Also, if we let people move into a house that needs work, we don't look very professional. This is why we have our handyman. We let him fix up our houses before the tenants move in.

Another way we try to keep our good tenants happy is with our rent increases. As we mentioned in the last chapter, responsible tenants get very good treatment from us when it's time to raise their rent. That doesn't mean their rent stays the same year after year. In fact, it goes up every single year, without fail. But we do it so reasonably and politely that we actually make the tenants feel grateful to us. We send them a letter like the one on page 149.

By the time a tenant finishes reading that letter, he feels good about himself and good about us. If he's upset at all, it's with the government, or the unions, or our nasty old accountant, but not with his landlords. We're the nice people who recognize what an exceptionally responsible, hardworking person he is, and we're so generous that we're actually giving him a present and helping him keep his rent as low as possible. How could a tenant resent landlords like that?

Once tenants prove themselves to us, we do everything reasonable to hold on to them. We don't want to rule all our tenants by fear. That keeps the bad ones in line and/or scares them away, but it does nothing to turn the good tenants into the kind of long-term, stable "employees" our company needs to thrive. In order to attract and hold those people, we have to do one more thing besides all the things we mentioned in this chapter. We have to maintain the property and keep it in good, livable shape. That's our part of the bargain, and it's also the subject of our next chapter.

RENT INCREASE LETTER FOR GOOD TENANTS

Dear Mr. and Mrs. Tenant:

Gee, is it a year already? Time sure does fly when you're not paying attention. The fact that it has gone by so fast shows that we all made the
right decision a year ago. You have been the kind of good, trouble-free tenants that we were looking for, and we hope you have been happy in your new
home.

After all the horror stories we have heard from other landlords, we really
appreciate having you in our house, and we want you to know that. Now that
you've been with us for a year, we look forward to having you join our family
of "preferred customers," and to celebrate your first anniversary, we are
going to give you the services of our handyman free for one day. He will
paint, clean, and/or make any minor repairs or improvements you would like.
This is to show you in a concrete, practical way how much we appreciate your
efforts to work with us and help us keep our costs down.

Just to let you know that we do appreciate the efforts you have made to
improve the property and make it a real home, we are going to forego our
standard ten percent yearly rent increase and make a special exception in
your case.

Believe me, we wish that we did not have to raise the rent at all, but our
accountant insists that we have no choice. Inflation is eating us up, and our
expenses are running way ahead of our income. Taxes and insurance costs are
up, along with the prices we pay for labor and materials to keep the property
properly maintained. We hate it at least as much as you do, but we need your
help and cooperation if we are going to hold on to the house and keep it up.

As I said earlier, our normal policy is to raise rents ten percent a year,
but we talked it over and decided to make a special exception in your case.
Therefore, we cut the increase down to the bare minimum we could live with.
We worked it all out and decided that we have to have at least a $_____
increase. There is just no way around it. While no one wants to pay more
rent, this means you'll be paying only $_____ as opposed to the $_____
you would be paying if we raised the rent the normal amount. Since you have
held up your end of the rental contract, we want to do all we can to uphold
ours.

We are enclosing a new discount rental agreement for you to sign. The rent
it calls for will be $_____, a $_____ increase over the official rent
you pay now, but you will of course continue to enjoy our $50.00 good-tenant
discount, so you will actually be paying only $_____. Please initial all
the pages and sign your full signature on the last page. Mail it back to us
and we will photocopy it and send a copy back to you with our signatures.

On the other hand, we know what it's like when your budget is strained to
the limit and you just can't afford any increased expenses at all. If this is
the position you're in and you decide not to stay with us, we wish you good
fortune in the future, and we will be pleased to provide references any time
you need one.

Please send the new rental agreement back as soon as possible and let us
know when you would like your handyman for a day.

Sincerely yours,

Michael J. Milin

Eleven

Property Maintenance

If you own rental property, you have to maintain it. Sooner or later, you'll have to deal with repairs. It's a fact of life you can't escape and when it happens, you have two choices: you can do the work yourself, or you an hire it out. Either way, it's got to get done and either way, it's going to cost you time and money, so be prepared.

Many landlords aren't prepared for problems when they come up. They aren't equipped to do the necessary repairs themselves and they don't know whom to call. This isn't the professional way to do things, and it isn't smart.

The first thing to do is analyze your own abilities and see if you really have the skill and/or the time to maintain the property yourself. Many people make the mistake of thinking that their own labor is free, but in most cases it isn't. If you could be using that time for some other, more profitable purpose, then it costs you money to spend the time doing your own maintenance. If nothing else, you could go out and work for some other landlord and get paid for it. Of course, if you enjoy working on property, that's okay. You can treat it as a hobby. But if you don't enjoy it, you should consider hiring someone else to do the work. Either way, you should figure in the cost of maintenance when you work out your expenses. Don't figure that you have a positive cash flow unless you have already put aside money for future repairs. You should put aside at least 5% of the income for this purpose.

In our case, the choice was clear. We have neither time nor desire to do our own repairs. We don't enjoy that kind of work, and we're too busy to do it even if we liked it. Our time is valuable. We earn far more per hour than we pay to the workers who do our maintenance for us. And we are frequently out of town, so we couldn't do much maintenance on our properties anyway. The only question is whom to hire.

HASSLE-FREE MAINTENANCE

We decided that we didn't want to hire full-time employees and put them on the payroll. It made much more sense to hire an independent contractor. This way we have almost no bookkeeping, and we aren't responsible for paying someone when there's no work. We pay our handyman by the job. Each time there's something to be done, we send him out to the property and he comes back to us with a bid. If we think we can get someone else to do the job for less, we're free to get other bids, but most of the time we stick with our regular man.

By using the same handyman again and again, we get the lowest price and the best service. He gets professional discounts on many materials, and passes at least some of that along to us. We know he'll always give us honest bids. Most of all, it simplifies things for us. And, as we mentioned before, by using one man all the time, we have a built-in watchguard system to keep tenants in line.

We hire specialists when we need them. There are certain things our handyman can't do, such as fixing stoves or putting on new roofs. But when it comes to ordinary maintenance— painting, carpentry, plumbing, et cetera—we use the handyman, and it works out a lot cheaper. Since he's an independent contractor, we have no liability. He has his own insurance, his own vehicle, his own equipment, and his own crew. He is an independent businessman, not our employee.

That makes a big difference if anything goes wrong. If there are any accidents, or if someone gets cheated (or thinks he did), it will be hard for anyone to sue us. It's all part of hassle-free management. You have to anticipate possible problems and head them off before they happen.

HEADING OFF PROBLEMS

We have our handyman check each one of our houses twice a year. Everything that needs to be replaced on a regular basis, such as cooler pads, is the responsibility of the tenant. It's all right there in the rental agreement; however, to make sure the tenants remember this, we send them letters such as those on the next two pages.

These precautions take care of most of our maintenance problems, but not all of them. We still get emergency calls when something breaks down. With one hundred houses, you can't avoid it. That's why we always keep repair money in reserve, although we don't believe in doing unnecessary repairs or improvements. This is a common mistake that many landlords make. They paint and freshen up a house every time a tenant moves out. They waste a lot of money this way, because many times repainting, or even cleaning, isn't necessary.

We hold our tenants responsible for leaving our houses in good condition when they move. Since the house is always in move-in condition when tenants move in, we expect it to be the same way when they move out. If it isn't, they pay for it out of their security deposits.

We don't change the carpets or repaint every time a new tenant moves (that's clearly stated in the rental contract, too). We try to keep our maintenance costs as low as posible and save our money for things that really need to be done. A leaky roof has to be fixed or it will damage the rest of the house, but no house was ever seriously damaged by an unpainted living room or bedroom. The time we save by not getting involved in unnecessary maintenance leaves us more time for the subject of our next chapter, cutting expenses. But in order to keep things running smoothly, we have to make sure our tenants do their part. Sample maintenance reminder letters for furnace and cooler maintenance are given on the two following pages.

LETTER TO TENANTS CONCERNING
FURNACE MAINTENANCE

October 11, 1982

Dear Tenant:

We will be closing down the coolers and starting up the furnaces now that the winter months are approaching.

In order for our program to be both successful and organized, we MUST have your cooperation. Please fill out the bottom portion of this letter and send back to us as soon as possible.

Wayne Anderson, our handyman, is scheduled to be in your area on _____(date)_____ to service the furnace. If there is a problem with this date, please indicate so on the return portion and we will try to reschedule your appointment at a future date.

We realize this is very short notice for some of you, but we ask for your cooperation.

Thank you,

Irene V. Milin

- -

Please return this portion

Name_____

Address _____

Phone (H)_____ (W)_____

I   will
    will not   be available on the date mentioned above to have
              my furnace serviced.

Send to   P.O. Box 17524
             Tucson, AZ 85731

We need this back <u>as soon as possible</u>, so please fill out and return immediately.

LETTER TO TENANTS CONCERNING
COOLER MAINTENANCE

April 9, 1983

Dear Tenant:

As the recent warm spell has reminded us, it is time to prepare the evaporative coolers for spring and summer use. The
proper maintenance of the cooling system will enable the coolers
to operate more efficiently and last longer.

Rather than waiting until the last minute, the owner of the
property has contracted Mr. Wayne Anderson to begin a routine
inspection of all coolers toward the latter part of February or
early March. The owner will provide the service at no charge.
The following services will be provided:

1. Scraping and cleaning of cooler panels and body.
2. Protective sealing and painting of cooler body (inside
   only).
3. Patching of minor leaks.
4. Adjustments of floats, water flow, and belt tension.
5. Oiling of motor bearings and squirrel cage bushings.
6. Labor on installation of pads.
7. Service call/<u>one</u> (1) <u>only</u> to adjust any of the above items
   during first two weeks of operation.

<u>This service does not cover the following and will be the re-
sponsibility of the tenant:</u>

1. Replacement of pumps, floats, drains, spiders, tubing,
   bearings, motors, belts and cords, or the labor required
   to install them.
2. Cost of pads.
3. Major patching of cooler body.
4. Repair of electrical components, switches, etc.

In the long run, proper maintenance will ensure lower costs
and will avoid any discomfort for you and your family during the
hot months.

Mr. Anderson will be in contact with you directly and will
book the appointments. Your cooperation is appreciated in this
matter.

Sincerely yours,

Irene V. Milin

**At the tenant's request, Mr. Anderson will be available to
service and provide parts that are not covered by the owner's
inspection service. Any costs incurred are the sole responsibility of the tenant. Furthermore, Mr. Anderson will stand
behind the products and service he personally provides.

Twelve

Cutting Expenses

A DOLLAR SAVED TIMES ONE HUNDRED PROPERTIES ADDS UP

We've learned that even small savings can make a big difference. With one hundred properties, we have to keep close tabs on expenses or our cash flow can vary widely. We've learned to put every dollar where it will count most and only there. We train our tenants to save money and it pays off. It's helped to make us millionaires.

Tenants are like anyone else: left to their own devices, they will do things the easy way. Unfortunately, that's not always the right way. It's not always the way that will be most economical. If that's the case, then you just have to break them of their old habits and teach them new ones. That's an important part of being a landlord.

Two Garbage Cans Aren't Better Than One

They are just twice as expensive. The tenants probably think it's better to have two cans per unit. That way, they won't have to exert themselves at all. That's fine, if they're paying for the garbage service. But if you're paying for it, then don't you think you should teach them to squash the trash bags with their feet, so they can get by with one can?

It sounds petty, doesn't it? You can't be bothered with something that silly, can you? We used to feel that way about a lot of things until we sat down and added it up. In our area, garbage service is cheap. It costs only 50¢ a week per pail, or a little over $2.00 per month per pail. For each pail we could eliminate, we would save $2.00 per month. With one hundred properties, that's about $450 per month. Plus, we eliminated the replacement cost of those extra pails. Each pail has to be replaced once a year, at an average cost of $9 per pail. By eliminating two hundred pails, we save another $1,800 a year, or $150 per month. Added to the $450 a month we save on collection services, this gives us a total savings of $600 per month. That is enough to rent a nice house or apartment in most areas. It is definitely enough to make payments on our expensive cars each month. Think about that the next time you see someone driving down the street in a Mercedes or a Jaguar and you wonder what they do to pay for a car like that. It could easily be you in the driver's seat. All you have to do is take control.

Lights Can Eat Up Your Profits

If you are paying for them, why should the tenants worry about shutting them off? It's nice to have light on outside your house or apartment all night. It provides a feeling of security. The electricity it consumes is minimal—until you start accumulating a few properties.

We have a firm rule: If we pay the bill, then we control the switch. We try to avoid paying for outside lights and little extras like that, but when we do pay, we make sure that we—not the tenants—control it. In fact, this is one more thing that makes smaller properties more attractive: often there are no outside lights or common areas to worry about and maintain.

We like to make the tenants as responsible as possible for the maintenance. That's the main thing that cuts costs. With our tenants acting as an on-site maintenance crew, serious problems don't have a chance to develop through neglect.

TRAINING A HANDYMAN

This takes time and effort, but it usually pays off in the long run. If the toilet goes out and you call a plumber, he will probably charge you $50 an hour. A good handyman might cost you $10 an hour. He will do the same job as the plumber. In fact, for your purposes, he might even be better if you've trained him properly.

A professional plumber won't necessarily be thinking of ways to save you money. If the handyman wants to keep working for you, he will. He will look for good used parts where they will work as well as new ones. He will look for shortcuts to cut the labor costs and he will tell the tenants to do it themselves when it turns out to be something minor. He will do all these things, because this is what you train him to do. Remember, when you're a landlord, nothing happens by accident. Accidents happen to people, but successful landlords don't wait for things to happen, they make them happen.

By keeping on top of your properties, your tenants, and your handyman, you will anticipate problems before they get out of hand. But cutting the little expenses will save you only so much. In order to really start reaping big benefits, you've got to start cutting big expenses.

ELIMINATE ALL EXPENSES THAT WILL INCREASE

The basic idea of building wealth through real estate is that your expenses are supposed to remain relatively fixed, while the income keeps growing. If you get bogged down with expenses that keep increasing each year, you are defeating yourself before you even start. Some expenses, like property taxes and assessments, you can't control. They are going to keep going up, whether you manage your property properly or not. But you can control your fate to a certain extent, by avoiding areas where the taxes are unusually high and/or are likely to go up in the future. Not all communities tax properties at the same rate. Some have a strong industrial and commercial base. Others depend on residential property for tax money. You can also eliminate the expenses that will really increase in the future, such as utilities. Utility costs are going up much faster than rents in most areas, so why should you want to pay for utilities? Even if it means accepting less rent, or spending a little bit of money to convert from a central furnace or electrical meter to individual units, do it.

With utility bills going up 25 percent to 100 percent a year in most areas, there is no way you can lose. Can you raise the rents 25 percent to 100 percent a year over the next few years? Probably not. And it means that you will be losing more and more money each time the cost of utilities goes up again.

You can get property improvement loans to cover the cost of converting the heat and electricity. The Department of Housing and Urban Development sponsors the Title I loan program, which makes money for repairs and improvements available through cooperating lenders. There are conventional and private second mortgages available as well. The immediate savings should cover the payments.

Cut Expenses Before You Buy the Property

You can do this by dealing with the seller. This comes back to buying right to own right. If your expenses are too high, then you won't be able to hold on to the property comfortably. Being a landlord should be a solution, not a problem.

Ask for a Moratorium on Payments

If you are taking over a property with known management problems, get the seller to carry a loan and then don't make any payments until you get the property operating on a profitable basis. Try for as long a moratorium as you can get: six months, a year, or even longer.

Of course you're going to have to pay that money back sooner or later, but you should be paying it back in inflated dollars and by then the income from the rents should be way up, so the property should pay that amount back for you.

Tie the Payments to the Property's Performance

Put the burden on the seller. If you make money from the property, then he makes money. If you don't make money, then neither does he. This works wonders when sellers try to inflate the value of their properties. Alas, not all sellers are honest all the time. Some of them will even lie about the amount of income they are taking in, or the amount of money that's going out to cover expenses. But they can't do that very effectively when your payments to them are based on the true figures.

Have the Seller Carry a Graduated-Payment Loan

With payments that start off lower than normal and then increase each year as the rents go up, you keep your expenses low and manageable in the beginning and you get a chance to cover the increases by raising the rents.

Get an Adjustable-Rate Loan

The interest rate starts off lower than normal and then goes up or down according to the dictates of the marketplace. In the long run, the interest rate is more likely to go up than down, but that shouldn't be a problem as long as you are raising the rents on a regular basis. The main advantage is that it makes the property affordable in the beginning, while the rents are low.

Get the Seller to Carry a Loan with Interest-Only Payments

That way you save the amount that would normally go toward reducing the principal. You will just have to pay that off in one lump sum when the loan term is up. This is the dreaded balloon payment you have probably heard about.

It is called a balloon payment because it blows up all at once. This can be dangerous, but there are safeguards you can take. First of all, never sign a note with a payoff date less than seven years down the road. This will give you plenty of time to decide how you are going to make the payoff, whether you are going to sell the property, refinance it, or pull cash from somewhere else.

Put a Backdoor Clause in All Your Notes

This is simply a clause that lets you extend the loan term if you are not ready to pay off the loan when it comes due. Usually, you will pay a penalty, say 10 percent of the outstanding balance, to exercise this privilege, but it gives you the flexibility you need to keep the balloon from popping in your face. Why be locked into an agreement that forces you to pay off the loan, even if market conditions, or conditions in your personal life, are not right? The only way to deal with balloon payments safely is to use some sort of backdoor clause. That way, no one can back you into a corner in the future and make you pay an exorbitant price to get out.

Have the Seller Carry a Note with No Payments

That way, you will keep your expenses as low as possible. If you're going to have a balloon payment anyway, you may as well do it right.

This is one of our favorite techniques. It not only keeps our monthly expenses low, it often gives us a chance to buy the note back at a discount later on. Sellers will often accept soft terms when they are anxious to be rid of the property, but then, once a little time has passed, they decide they really need the cash. We always have a first right of refusal clause in all our notes. If the sellers decide to sell any of those notes, we have the first right to make an offer before anyone else does.

In many cases, we are able to buy back our notes for 50 percent to 60 percent of the face value. How much money do we save this way? A lot. We get into most of our properties with no money down and keep our monthly expenses low by not making any payments to the sellers on the notes they carry. Then, when we can buy the notes back at a discount, we save even more money.

But saving money is only part of the overall plan. Ultimately, you want to make money—enough money to let you retire without suffering a change in your life-style and your standard of living. To do that, you have to have a handle on the bookkeeping and that's the subject of our next chapter.

Thirteen

Bookkeeping

You can't build up a real estate empire if you don't know how to keep the books. Buying and selling, wheeling and dealing are the fun parts. Even dealing with tenants and/or maintenance can be an enjoyable challenge.

Bookkeeping, on the other hand, is just plain work. But what's the point of making money if you can't keep track of how fast it's coming in, or where it's going on its way out? How will you ever know if you're making a profit?

We were not math or accounting majors in college and we're not exactly fond of bookkeeping today. We would much rather be out there buying properties from sellers at a discount, or giving lectures at seminars and conventions. We even prefer interviewing tenants to doing the bookkeeping. Since we don't enjoy bookkeeping any more than anyone else does, we try to make it as simple as possible. We don't want to spend any more time on it than we absolutely have to. Bookkeeping doesn't make us any money—it just helps us keep track of what we've got. Have you ever tried to keep track of more than one hundred mortgage payments each month without having some sort of system? We have to be organized. We have no choice.

GETTING YOUR MONEY COMES FIRST

The first problem, of course, is making sure we have an income. If we have one hundred mortgage payments going out each month on single-family houses, then ideally, we should also have one hundred rent checks coming in. That's our main priority: seeing that the money comes in smoothly and on time each month. Most of our tenants just bring their rent into the office each month to make sure that it isn't late. We stress the fact that the rent is due *in our office* by the first. If the tenants don't bring it in person, it's their problem if it comes in late. They will lose their discount.

We give our tenants preaddressed envelopes so they can mail their rent to our office if they want to, but they have to mail it before the first in order to get it to us in time. The burden is on them. We just set the rules, and it's up to the tenants to figure out how to avoid breaking them.

If you don't have an office, you'll probably have to give your tenants envelopes, too. After all, you don't want them coming to your house, do you? You should get yourself a post office box and maintain your privacy. Since we do have an office, we encourage our tenants to bring their rent in. This helps us establish a personal but businesslike relationship with them—on our terms. It's one more way of keeping an eye on the tenants, and it encourages them to pay promptly.

Automatic Rent Transfers

Whenever possible, we get our tenants to bank where we do. This way their rent money can automatically be transferred from their accounts right to our account each month. It also gives us a good relationship with our banker. Since we bring him so many new customers, we get special treatment in return.

You can also set up a collection account with a bank, savings and loan, or title or escrow company. This way the tenant's rent money is deposited in your account and then your mortgage payments, taxes, and insurance are automatically paid. You can even have the tenant's bank deduct the rent money from his checking or savings accounts and transferred to your account even if you don't use the same bank. There might be a fee involved, but the tenant pays that.

One successful investor we know won't rent to anyone whose bank won't go along with this arrangement. We aren't quite that radical. As long as we get our money on time, we don't care if the tenants mail it in, bring it in person, or deposit it directly into our account. The important thing to know is how much you're supposed to be getting each month and how it usually comes in. We know which tenants usually bring their rent in, which ones mail it in, and which ones usually deposit it right into the bank.

Each month we check with the bank to see which deposits have come in, we check the mail, and we check the traffic through our office. The rent is due by five o'clock. If we don't have it by three, we start calling people to remind them they they'll lose their discount if the rent isn't in by closing time.

That's how we *get* our money, but it doesn't explain how we keep track of it. You can't call a tenant and demand your rent if you aren't even sure whether it's been paid or not. You have to have accurate records of what's come in and what's gone out, who owes you money, and whom you owe money to.

A SIMPLE SYSTEM

If you have more than a few properties, separate checking accounts for each of them can be a problem. How do you keep all those checks straight? What do you do about all the different deposits? Can you imagine what it would be like to deal with one hundred different checking accounts?

What do you do if, like us, you work with investors, using other people's money to buy houses? How would you go about handling all those different houses owned by all those different people?

As we've said, we have more than one hundred houses in Tucson plus a few more in California. Fortunately, we've found a system that almost takes care of itself. We took an excellent property investment seminar taught by two men named Charles Green and Dennis Koelsch. They taught us about a system called Property Management D-12. This is a commercial bookkeeping package put out by Safeguard Business Systems. It's available from local distributors in most areas of the country, and there are also similar bookkeeping systems from other companies that are often just as good. There is nothing mystical or innovative about it. It's just simple and efficient.

The Property Card

Property Management D-12 is basically a one-entry pegboard system. You start with two cards for each property that you own or manage. The first one is the property card. You write down the address of the property and the name of the owner, whether it's you or an investor. You also write down all the vital information about the property. What are the loans? What interest rates are they at, and who holds them? What are the monthly payments?

You should include information on your insurance coverage for that property. Write down the name of your insurance company, the mailing address, and the 800 number to call in case you have a problem. Of course, you also need the name of your local insurance agent and his address and phone number. If you have problems with the company, your agent will intervene on your behalf.

If you bought the property through a real estate agent, then his name, address, and phone number should be on the property card. And don't forget the legal description of the property, the assessor's parcel number and any other tax information, such as what the semiyearly installments are and when they are due. Are taxes included in your monthly payments? Note this on the card, too.

The first card should contain a complete property record, just as the name implies. It should also list the property's tax code number, the assessor's separate valuations for the land and the improvement (the house), and beneficiary statements from any and all lenders detailing the exact status of all loans against the property as of a certain date. (The beneficiary statement should state exactly how much remains owing, what the terms of the loan are, the interest rate, due date, and so on, including an amortization table showing how much interest you will be paying over the life of the loan.)

The Ledger Card

The second card you need for each property is the ledger card. This is where you enter all financial transactions pertaining to that property, all deposits to and withdrawals from that property's account. That way you can pinpoint your exact income and expenditures at a glance.

Property Codes

What makes the card system work is the code system that goes with it. Each property gets its own code number. You write this on both the ledger card and the property card. This helps you to identify each property quickly without having to look up the street address. You have the tenants write this code number on their checks or money orders, and you write it on the check each time you pay a bill connected with that property. You can number your properties in sequence, 1-2-3-4-5 . . . , or you can use only odd numbers, such as 1-3-5-7 . . . or number them any way you like. The purpose of the code is not secrecy, but convenience and ease of organization.

USING THE SYSTEM

For example, let's say that rent money has come in for twenty-five of your houses all at once. You go to your ledger card file and get out the ledger cards for those twenty-five houses. Each check has a code number—for instance, 15—written on it. You pull out the ledger card with the same code number 15. It will also be cross-referenced according to the street address and the owner's name. Then you get out the ledger for your business checking account and line it up with the property cards.

You enter the tenant's name, the date, and the amount of rent money he has paid on the property card. A piece of carbon paper automatically copies it on the appropriate line of the ledger. Then you write the code number for the property next to it on the same line.

The property coded with number 15 is located at One Cross Road. Your files are cross-referenced so that you can locate the property by looking under the number 15, the property address One Cross Road, or the owner's name, Ina Index.

When you write the information about the tenant's rent payment in the ledger, you're doing two things. You are adding the amount of the rent payment to the overall amount in your business checking account, and you are also adding that amount to the account for One Cross Road, house number 15. For example, let's say the rent on One Cross Road is $350 a month. You would add $350 to the general total in your business checking account. Let's say that would increase the amount from $12,000 to $12,350.

You would also add that same $350 to the account for One Cross Road. Let's say there's $300 in that account. This boosts it to $650. That's the nice thing about the system. You can tell not only how much money you are taking in, but where it's coming from. Which properties are bringing in the most rent?

You can also see how much money is going out, and also where it's going. You can see which properties are costing you the most for negative cash flow, repairs, lost rent, and other expenses. This way you can use one checking account for many different properties and not get confused.

EXPENSE CODES

The Safeguard system also breaks expenses down into code numbers. For instance, number 14 stands for mortgage payments and number 12 stands for taxes. So when you write out the mortgage check for One Cross road, you would write 15 for property code in the ledger and 14 for expense code, and you would write both numbers on the check. That way you know later that the $300 check you wrote on April 1, 1983, was for the first mortgage payment for One Cross road. If it was a payment on a second mortgage, it would be listed under a different expense code number, say 13. Examples are on the following pages.

This would tell you all you need to know: whom to charge the expense to, which owner and which property, and what the money was for. If a question ever comes up about the first mortgage payment for One Cross Road for April 1983, the information will all be there. In fact, you will have two copies of

PROPERTY NAME _____

PROPERTY LOCATION _____

SUPERINTENDENT _____

PHONE _____

PROPERTY CODE _____

CARD NO. _____

REF NUMBER	PAID TO	DATE	CODE PROP	CODE DISB.	PERIOD ENDING	DEPOSITS	CHECK AMOUNT	NEW BALANCE

Safeguard
BUSINESS SYSTEMS, U.S.A.

PROPERTY INCOME AND DISBURSEMENT RECORD

DISBURSEMENT ACCOUNT CODES

OWNERS
01 Withdrawals
02 Reserve Savings
03 Reserve Investments
04
05
06
07
08
09 Other

MORTGAGES & LOANS
11 First Mortgage
12 Second Mortgage
13 Third Mortgage
14 Bank Loans
15 Bank Loan Interest
16 Other Loans
17 Other Loan Interest
18
19 Other

CAPITAL IMPRVMTS
21 Stoves & Refrigs
22 Air Conditioners
23 Furniture
24 Building
25 Roof
26 Furnace
27
28
29 Other

TAXES & LICENSES
31 Escrow
32 Real Estate
33 Personal Property
34 Withholding & FICA
35 Unemployment Comp
36 Licenses & Permits
37
38
39 Other

REPAIRS
41 Payroll (Net)
42 Appliances
43 Carpentry
44 Electrical
45 Painting
46 Plumbing
47 Elevator
48 Heating
49 Other

MAINTENANCE
51 Payroll (Net)
52 Refuse
53 Grounds
54 Supplies
55
56
57
58
59 Other

UTILITIES
61 Oil
62 Electricity
63 Gas
64 Telephone
65 Water
66
67
68
69 Other

PROFESSIONAL
71 Legal
72 Accounting
73 Architect
74 Management
75
76
77
78
79 Other

INSURANCE
81 Package
82 Fire
83 Liability
84 Compensation
85 Fidelity
86 Auto
87
88
89 Other

MISCELLANEOUS
91 Advertising
92 Rental Fees
93 Sec Deposit Refund
94 Rent Deposit Refund
95 Postage
96
97
98
99 Other

	PROPERTY NAME	Mike & Irene Milin				PROPERTY CODE	#35	
	PROPERTY LOCATION	4656 S. Rossette				CARD NO.	1	
	SUPERINTENDENT							
		PHONE						

REF NUMBER	PAID TO	DATE	CODE PROP	CODE DISB.	PERIOD ENDING	DEPOSITS	CHECK AMOUNT	NEW BALANCE 200 00
	First Interstate Bank	1/01/84	35	11	Jan. mtg.		172 93	27 07
	Jan Collins	1/01/84	35		Jan. rent	400 —		427 07
	First Interstate Bank	2/01/84	35	11	Feb. mtg.		172 93	254 14
	Jan Collins	2/01/84	35		Feb. rent	400 —		654 14
	Mike & Irene Milin	2/05/84	35	01	proceeds		454 14	200 —
	Tucson Newspapers	2/21/84	35	91	advertising		12 12	187 88
	Tucson Electric Power	2/26/84	35	62	elec. bill		7 13	180 75
	First Interstate Bank	3/01/84	35	11	March mtg.		172 93	7 82
	Larry Johnson	3/01/84	35		March rent	425 —		432 82
	Mike & Irene Milin	3/05/84	35	01	proceeds		232 82	200 —
	First Interstate Bank	4/01/84	35	11	April mtg.		172 93	27 07
	Larry Johnson	4/01/84	35		April rent	425 —		452 07
	Tucson Electric	4/12/84	35	62	closing bill		6 19	445 88
	First Interstate Bank	5/01/84	35	11	May mtg.		172 93	272 95
	Larry Johnson	5/01/84	35		May rent	425 —		697 95
	Mike & Irene Milin	5/05/84	35	01	proceeds		597 95	100 —

Safeguard
BUSINESS SYSTEMS, U.S.A.

PROPERTY INCOME AND DISBURSEMENT RECORD

DISBURSEMENT ACCOUNT CODES

OWNERS	MORTGAGES & LOANS	CAPITAL IMPRVMTS	TAXES & LICENSES	REPAIRS	MAINTENANCE	UTILITIES	PROFESSIONAL	INSURANCE	MISCELLANEOUS
01 Withdrawals	11 First Mortgage	21 Stoves & Refrigs	31 Escrow	41 Payroll (Net)	51 Payroll (Net)	61 Oil	71 Legal	81 Package	91 Advertising
02 Reserve Savings	12 Second Mortgage	22 Air Conditioners	32 Real Estate	42 Appliances	52 Refuse	62 Electricity	72 Accounting	82 Fire	92 Rental Fees
03 Reserve Investments	13 Third Mortgage	23 Furniture	33 Personal Property	43 Carpentry	53 Grounds	63 Gas	73 Architect	83 Liability	93 Sec. Deposit Refund
04	14 Bank Loans	24 Building	34 Withholding & FICA	44 Electrical	54 Supplies	64 Telephone	74 Management	84 Compensation	94 Rent Deposit Refund
05	15 Bank Loan Interest	25 Roof	35 Unemployment Comp	45 Painting	55	65 Water	75	85 Fidelity	95 Postage
06	16 Other Loans	26 Furnace	36 Licenses & Permits	46 Plumbing	56	66	76	86 Auto	96
07	17 Other Loan Interest	27	37	47 Elevator	57	67	77	87	97
08	18	28	38	48 Heating	58	68	78	88	98
09 Other	19 Other	29 Other	39 Other	49 Other	59 Other	69 Other	79 Other	89 Other	99 Other

it, one in your business checking account ledger and one on the property card for One Cross Road.

When you've made all your entries, the property cards go back into a property file. The file on One Cross road, for instance, would also contain the original purchase contract for the house, the closing papers from the title company, and a copy of the structural pest control report, as well as any other inspection reports.

Computers are the wave of the future. Why do boring work when a machine can do it much better? *Time* magazine didn't name the computer the man of the year for no reason. If you plan to have a rental operation of any size, you should seriously look into buying one. Bookkeeping scares too many people away from real estate investing, and it keeps others from expanding. There is no reason for this. Bookkeeping is no fun, but with or without a computer, it can be licked. It's not an insurmountable problem, and neither is the subject of our next chapter, taxes.

Fourteen

How to Save Money on Taxes

Aside from the fact that it's one of the best inflation-proof investments available, real estate has always been a good tax shelter. If you own enough real estate, you can avoid paying taxes at all. You can do it legally, safely, and without resorting to any complicated or risky schemes. Real estate always has value because everyone needs a place to live. Do they really need pork bellies or bull semen or dried-up oil wells? These tax shelters come and go. Real estate is more than a fad.

But it's one thing to know that real estate offers tremendous tax benefits and it's another thing to take full advantage of those benefits. In order to get everything you're entitled to, you have to plan ahead.

You should always consult a professional, such as a tax attorney, real estate attorney, or experienced accountant if you have any questions. We are not tax professionals offering legal advice, but we do want to tell you what we've learned and share some of our experiences.

BUY RIGHT TO PAY TAXES RIGHT

Real estate offers many different tax advantages, and there are many ways to use the tax laws, depending on your situation. The amount of money you are making, the amount you expect to make in the future, your intended use for the property, and how long you intend to keep it will all have an effect on the way you treat the property for tax purposes. Do you take straight-line or accelerated depreciation? Do you use component depreciation, and if so, how do you figure the value of the components? How do you figure in the value of the nondepreciable land?

There's a lot of money at stake and a lot of decisions to be made. If you buy certain types of properties and use them for low-income housing, you can get increased write-offs. If you do certain types of work to your property, it qualifies as repairs and can all be written off in one year. Other types of expenditures are considered improvements. These have to be depreciated.

Whenever possible, we try to take all these factors into account before we buy a house. We believe in tax write-offs. They're a major benefit, if not *the* major benefit, of owning property nowadays.

Investment Strategies Change

In many areas people don't buy real estate to get income anymore—especially not single-family houses. The rents won't even cover the expenses in most cases, and people are ecstatic if they can break even instead of losing money each month. Inflation is nice—when it happens. But there has been very little inflation since 1981 and obviously you can't always count on it. In the best times, real estate doesn't appreciate at a steady, even pace. It goes up in fits and starts. It hits plateaus and the prices level off or even drop a little. It can stay that way for years. Who knows when houses will really start to go up in value again? Who knows if they will ever go up at 15 percent to 20 percent a year again? No one can really predict what will happen. But tax benefits will go on. Tax laws will change. Things will get better and things will get worse, but owning real estate will always give you tax benefits.

Why? Because the government wants you to buy rental property. It's good for the country. Just as businesspeople are given tax breaks that wage earners don't enjoy, landlords get benefits that tenants can't. The reason for this is that business owners and landlords are part of the creative force that keeps our economy going. Tenants and salaried employees don't contribute nearly as much. Businesspeople employ other people. They create jobs and generate tax money. Landlords provide shelter for people who would not otherwise be able to provide it for themselves.

Society needs people who are willing to take on these jobs, so it rewards them with tax benefits. If you have ever run a business or been a landlord, then you know that they are both demanding, time-consuming jobs. It's a lot easier to be a tenant or an employee. Striking out on your own is hard. Taking on responsibility for others is even harder. This is why all sorts of credits and incentives are written into the tax laws to stimulate certain areas of the economy. This is also why low-income housing qualifies for special benefits that you can't get with ordinary real estate. It is why only income-producing property qualifies for depreciation at all.

You can't depreciate your own home or a piece of raw land. You can depreciate only a property that can be rented for housing or for business use. You can't even depreciate land that holds a building which is rented for housing or business use. You can only depreciate the building itself. Does this tell you anything about where you want to buy real estate or what kind of real estate you want to buy? Obviously, you don't want to buy raw land if you're seeking tax write-offs, but it goes a lot deeper than that and gets a lot more complex.

PREPARE FOR MAXIMUM DEPRECIATION

All other things being equal, you want to buy property in areas where lots sell cheaply in relation to houses. This way you can get the maximum tax benefits. More of your purchase price will be credited to depreciable improvements and less to nondepreciable land.

For example, let's say you have two $60,000 houses. One is in an area where building lots sell for about $10,000. The other house is in an area where lots are scarce, but available lots generally sell for $15,000 to $20,000. If everything else about the properties is roughly equal, the house on the $10,000 lot is the better buy, since it will give you an extra $5,000 to $10,000 of depreciable property.

We look at things like this when we consider a house. Of course, it isn't the primary consideration. Often areas where lots sell too cheaply have one serious drawback: property doesn't appreciate as quickly as it does in other areas. The lots are cheaper because the area isn't considered as desirable as it would be in another location. But this isn't always the case. Sometimes an area will have mostly inexpensive lots because they're harder to build on. For example, if the area is hilly or uneven, expensive foundations may be needed. This makes it more expensive to build on those sites, and so it lowers their value. However, it doesn't necessarily lower the value of the finished houses. They might appreciate at the same rate as comparable houses on less expensive lots. They might even appreciate faster, since hill areas are often reserved for the well-to-do who can afford to pay for a view.

LAND-TO-IMPROVEMENTS RATIO

How do you find out what the average land-to-improvements ratio is for the area? You go to a title company or to the county recorder's office and check the files. You look up all raw land sales in the area for the past year or two to establish a basis for valuing the land.

When you have these figures in hand, you check the records for sales of improved property. Find out how much the average house in the area has sold for over the last year or two. Subtract the average sale price for lots from the average sale price for houses, and you have a rough idea of what the breakdown for land and improvements will be for that area. This way, you know about how much tax write-off you can expect to get from any given house.

For example, we run our study on land costs and we discover that on the north side of town the average price for a building lot is $12,000. Houses in the area range all the way from $40,000 to $70,000, and for the last two years they've been going up at the rate of 5 percent per year. Lots have gone up 10 percent a year over the past two years.

Over on the south side, the average lot is going for $20,000 and the houses run from $60,000 to $80,000. The houses on the south side have also gone up about 5 percent a year over the last two years, but the lots haven't gone up at all. They seem to have peaked for a while.

We have to decide between two houses. One is a three-bedroom on the north side, and it's selling for $60,000. It will rent for about $400 a month. The other house is a three-bedroom house on the south side of town selling for $70,000. It rents for $500 a month. That extra $100 a month will just about cover the cost of paying an extra $10,000 for the house, so the cash flow on the houses should be about the same.

The appreciation on a $70,000 house might be slightly more than the appreciation on a $60,000 house, but that shouldn't be a big factor, since both houses are appreciating at the same rate. You're talking about a difference of approximately $500 a year. The fact that lots on the north side are still appreciating in value at 10 percent a year, while those on the south side haven't gone up in value in the last two years, could be a more significant factor. This could mean that the north side is becoming more popular and that property values for houses will begin going up faster, too.

We've still left out one factor of this equation, however, and that's the replacement cost of the houses. If the houses are harder to build on the north side because the lots are steeper, this means the replacement cost should be greater on the north side. A $60,000 house on the north side might actually cost as much or even more to replace than a $70,000 house on the south side. Replacement cost can be a strong argument on your side. If the replacement cost is higher, then the land value must be lower. A greater percentage of the purchase price should be allocated to the building and a smaller percentage to the land.

Finding Replacement Costs

Figuring the replacement cost of the building will be harder than figuring the value of the land. You can't just go to a title company or the recorder's office and look up sales records. You have to talk to builders and contractors and get figures from them. If you can get figures from them in writing, they may or may not be acceptable to the IRS.

You can also get standard reference books—perhaps in your local library—that will tell you the expected replacement costs for certain types of houses. These books will take into account the area, the style of house, and the materials used, and give you an average replacement cost. What they obviously can't do is take into account any special circumstances that might raise the replacement cost and, therefore, give you more tax deductions. In cases where you think that the replacement cost should be considered higher than normal, you should probably get a professional appraisal.

Hiring a professional to appraise a single-family house can run you anywhere from $65 to $150 depending on where you live, whom you call, and how detailed an appraisal you need. It can be well worth every penny of it. It's one thing to go into a tax audit and make claims about the land-to-improvement ratio and what it should be. It's something else to be able to prove your claims, and the appraiser can help you do that.

He's a disinterested expert with no real stake in your property or your tax claims. He is paid a flat fee, whether you win your audit or not. He isn't like a tax adviser who might be paid a percentage of anything you save. Therefore, the IRS will usually accept an appraiser's evaluation without challenging it, assuming, of course, that you used a qualified professional appraiser.

Working with an Appraiser

Check your state regulations first. If appraisers have to be licensed in your state, that makes it easy for you to find a qualified professional. Practically anyone who has a license should meet state standards. If they don't have to be licensed, then you should make sure your appraiser belongs to one of the recognized appraisal societies. Otherwise, the appraisal might not stand up in an audit.

The two main professional groups for real estate appraisers are the Appraiser's Institute, whose members are referred to as MAI (Member of the Appraiser's Institute) Appraisers, and the

Society of Real Estate Appraisers, SREA. There are also local and regional organizations, but those are the two organizations whose members are recognized nationwide. They have to pass rigorous tests to be admitted for membership, so you know they're qualified. They may charge a little bit more than an appraiser who doesn't hold either of these designations, but it could be well worth the extra charge to avoid an argument with the IRS.

Although the appraiser is supposed to be an impartial professional, it doesn't hurt to help him along with his job. If you have any comparables, replacement-cost figures, or other information that you feel would be useful, bring them to the appraiser's attention. You're the one paying for the appraisal, and you want one that will benefit you by lowering your tax bill. The appraiser won't lie or distort the facts just to help you, but figures can be used in many ways. If an appraiser has more figures than he needs—i.e., eight comparables when he has room for only three of them on his appraisal form—it's natural for him to use the ones that are most favorable to his client. That isn't cheating; it's just smart business.

That's why it's smart business for you to supply the appraiser with everything he needs to establish a high value on the improvements and a low value on the land. Get all the comparables you can, and sift through them to find the ones that help you the most. Pass those on to the appraiser and throw away the rest. Find out all you can about replacement cost. Talk to builders, contractors, and people who do remodeling. Get estimates from them and pass these on to the appraiser. Use sources who do quality work at premium prices, not those who mass-produce cheap housing.

If you provide the appraiser with good accurate information, why should he look for other information to contradict it? That's a waste of his time and effort, so he'll use your figures unless he has a good reason not to.

Personal Property Depreciation

You may also want to get separate appraisals for personal property associated with the operation of the rental property such as stoves, refrigerators, washers, dryers, storage sheds, and lawn equipment. Since the minimum depreciation schedule for the building itself is 27.5 years, while most of the personal property can be depreciated in seven years or less, personal property depreciation can save you a lot. In fact, it is a good idea to break down your purchase offers so that you specify all the personal property and put a value on each item right in the offer. This can sometimes be a good negotiating technique as well as a tax-saving measure. It often intimidates the seller.

TAKING RISKS

Almost everything we've talked about so far in this chapter and almost everything we will be talking about, is an extension of our subject for the previous chapter: bookkeeping. That's what it comes down to. You can do anything you want to avoid taxes —until you get caught.

You can credit 99 percent of the property value to the improvements and only 1 percent to the land. Then you can depreciate the property over two or three years. You don't even have to report the income when you sell a property. You can keep it all and pay no taxes on your profit, and no one will ever know —unless you get audited. But if you do get audited, you had better have records documenting all your expenses.

You'd also better be able to justify allocating your improvements at such a high ratio and then depreciating them so quickly. If you can prove your case, and if your accountant and attorney stand behind you, then more power to you. But you're going to need excellent records of every single detail of all your transactions, because the IRS will pull them apart to the last decimal point.

That's what we want to cover in the rest of this chapter: what records you have to keep and why. Knowing what deductions you can take and what the requirements and possible repercussions are is the first step. You have to know what deductions and write-offs are available, and then see which ones apply to your own situation.

THE OLD TAX LAW

Prior to 1982 the usable life span of income-producing real estate was generally considered to be thirty years for older properties and forty years for brand-new ones. There were exceptions—for example, some low-income housing rehabilitation projects could be depreciated in five years—but this was the general rule.

The general rule was set by the IRS. If you were audited and you claimed thirty-year depreciation on your older buildings and forty years on your new ones, you knew that the IRS would never challenge you in their audit. Thousands of people have depreciated their rental properties over twenty years, or even ten years. They have never been audited, so they never had any trouble. Others have been audited and have had to pay interest and penalties on all the back taxes due.

Then there is a third group, small but very real, who have beaten the IRS at its own game. They have depreciated their property in less than thirty years, they have been audited, and they have won. That's because they were prepared. They walked into the audit with everything—facts, figures, appraisers' evaluations, contractors' estimates—and were able to prove they were entitled to every penny they deducted.

THE NEW TAX LAW

The 1986 Tax Reform Act brought substantial changes to the tax code as it relates to real estate. Despite what some Prophets of Doom might lead you to believe, real estate remains an excellent tax-cutting investment vehicle for most people. It still provides deductions against income and tax credits that can translate into nice savings on your tax bill. Prior to tax reform, real estate tax benefits were exceptional. Now they are simply excellent.

Depreciation

Newly purchased residential income-producing real estate must be depreciated over 27.5 years using the straight-line method. Accelerated depreciation methods are no longer allowed. If you owned the property before the tax law changed, you should still use the depreciation method that was in effect at the time of purchase. Commercial real estate (i.e., office buildings, shopping centers, etc.) purchased after January 1, 1987, must be depreciated over 31.5 years, again on a straight-line basis.

You are still not allowed to use component depreciation for the building itself, claiming the roof and the electrical system and the plumbing as separate components. The whole building must be deducted as one unit over 27.5 years or more. But you can depreciate personal property associated with the operation of the rental unit. Items such as stoves, refrigerators, washers, dryers, and other equipment associated with the property can be depreciated over seven years instead of 27.5 years. But you have to do one of two things, as we stated before: Either write the value of each item into the purchase contract or get an appraisal of each item by a professional appraiser.

So, depreciation was hit pretty hard. Still the changes are not horrible, especially when you consider that we had thirty-year depreciation for years prior to 1982. Also, keep in mind that the value of your property is going up, even though the IRS allows you to take a depreciation allowance for the deterioration or wearing out of the property. And while the property appreciates, you don't pay a dime of taxes on that appreciation until you sell.

Capital Gains

Before tax reform, only 40 percent of the net long-term capital gains (profits) from the sale of real estate were taxable. Sixty percent of the gain went right into your pocket. Under tax reform, 100% of the gain is added to your income and taxed at the appropriate rate—depending on your tax bracket.

Passive Losses

Another major change in the tax law involves losses from a "passive trade or business activity." In the past, investors could use all losses from their investments to offset income from other sources. Now, if a loss is considered "passive" it may be used only to offset income from another "passive trade or business activity" and cannot be deducted against other sources of income such as salary, dividends, interest or capital gains. This comes as a large blow to many investors who depended on passive tax shelters with large write-offs to reduce their taxable income.

Fortunately, the passive loss rule applies to real estate activities in a special way. You can still deduct real estate losses against income from other sources provided you meet one important condition: You must "actively participate" in your real estate activities. "Actively participate" in real estate doesn't necessarily mean "regular, continuous and substantial" involvement in operations, it simply means that you genuinely participate in the making of management decisions.

For example, let's say you own a four-plex. You can still hire a residential property manager who will locate tenants and arrange for repairs or other services that the property requires. As long as you approve the tenants, set the terms for the lease, and approve the amounts of money that are to be paid for repairs, then you are "actively participating" in your real estate rental activity, even if you never show the apartment or personally call the repair man.

However, involvement in a tax-shelter real estate limited partnership is not considered "active participation." As a limited partner you are not allowed to participate in the operation of the property. A limited partnership is an obvious "passive trade or business activity."

If you are actively involved in the operations of a rental property then you are allowed to deduct up to $25,000 worth of losses from that property against your income. If you have more than $25,000 in losses in a particular year, the excess can be used to offset "passive" income, or else it can be carried forward to be used in future years. The $25,000 annual deduction is phased out for individuals with adjusted gross income of $100,000 to $150,000 per year. If your adjusted gross income is $150,000 or more, the $25,000 rule doesn't apply to you at all and all of your real estate losses are subject to the pasive loss rule.

Exactly how these rules will be applied is up to the tax courts.

However, one thing is clear: if you turn the whole operation over to a management company and say, "Just send me a check after all the bills are paid," then you are not an active participant.

Rehabilitation Tax Credits

If you restore a certified historic property, the IRS will let you take 20 percent of the rehabilitation costs as a tax credit. For example, if you spend $50,000 rehabilitating an historic property you can reduce your tax bill with a tax credit for $10,000. If the property is not certified historic, but was built before 1936, you are allowed a tax credit for 10 percent of the rehabilitation costs.

As an incentive to provide housing for persons with low incomes, the IRS will let investors take a 9 percent tax credit for new construction and rehabilitation costs on a low to moderate income housing. This tax credit is available to most investors unless the rehabilitation project is funded by a government subsidy, then the tax credit is reduced to four percent.

NEUTRALIZING NEGATIVE CASH FLOW

For now, let's see how these tax benefits can affect a negative cash flow property that you hold for five years. We'll take two scenarios: in one we buy a $60,000 house with $12,000 down; in the other, we buy it with none of our own cash.

The property is free and clear and the seller wants all cash, so we put down $12,000 and get a $48,000 loan at 11 percent. Our payments will be $457.12 a month. Of this amount, approximately $440.00 is interest and $17.12 goes toward the principal. This means we write off $440.00 a month, or $5,280 a year.

The property taxes will be about $780 a year, or $65 a month, and insurance will be about $275 a year, or $23 a month. All together, we'll be paying about $545 a month.

The problem is that the house will rent for only $495. This means we lose $50 a month, or $600 a year. Since we're in the 28 percent tax bracket and can write all of this off as a business loss, the government will be picking up part of the tab. We'll really lose only $36 a month, or $432 a year, out of our pockets, but we'll still be losing.

It looks something like this:

Purchase Price	$60,000	
Down Payment	$12,000	
New First Loan	$48,000 at 11%	$457/mo.
Taxes and Insurance		$ 88/mo.
Total Expenses		$545/mo.
Total Rental Income		$495/mo.
Negative Cash Flow		$ 50/mo.

If we bought the property for no money down, the story would be even worse. If we get the same $48,000 loan at 11 percent and have the seller carry a $12,000 second mortgage with interest-only payments at 10 percent per annum, our payment will be approximately $645 a month, instead of $545. We will now have a negative cash flow of about $150 a month.

It looks like this:

Purchase Price	$60,000	
New First Loan	$48,000 at 11%	$457/mo.
Seller Carries	$12,000 at 10%	
Second	(interest only)	$100/mo.
Taxes and Insurance		$ 88/mo.
Total Expenses		$645/mo.
Total Rental Income		$495/mo.
Negative Cash Flow		$150/mo.

We'll lose $1,800 the first year, and we can write 28 percent of that off, so we actually have to take $1,468 out of our pockets to subsidize the property—or do we? Assuming that we allow $8,850 for the value of the land, we would be able to depreciate $51,150 worth of improvements.

Assuming that we bought the property in January of 1988, we could take $1,860 as our depreciation allowance for the first year. We spent a total of $1,800 subsidizing the property for one year, and as a result, we saved $1,023 on our taxes. The property actually only cost us $65.00 a month. Not bad for a no-money-down deal. If the property was bought at a good discount, and can be sold for $68,000 to $70,000 in five years, then the deal is even better.

Here's what both properties look like for the first year:

Illustration One—Year One

Purchase Price	$60,000	
Land Value	$ 8,850	
Improvements Value	$51,150	
First Loan	$48,000 at 11%	$457/mo.
Down Payment	$12,000	
Taxes and Insurance		$ 88/mo.
Total Expenses	$6,540/yr.	$545/mo.
Total Rental Income	$5,940/yr.	$495/mo.
Negative Cash Flow	$ 600/yr.	$ 50/mo.
Depreciation	$1,860/yr.	$155/mo.
Loss for Tax Purposes	$2,460	$205/mo.
Tax Bracket	28%	
Total Tax Savings	$ 688/yr.	

Illustration Two—Year One

Purchase Price	$60,000	
First Loan	$48,000 at 11%	$457/mo.
Second Loan	$12,000 at 10%	
Carried by Seller	(interest only)	$100/mo.
Taxes and Insurance		$ 88/mo.
Total Expenses	$7,740/yr.	$645/mo.
Total Rental Income	$5,940/yr.	$495/mo.
Negative Cash Flow	$1,800/yr.	$150/mo.
Depreciation	$1,860/yr.	$155/mo.
Loss for Tax Purposes	$3,660	$305/mo.
Tax Bracket	28%	
Total Tax Savings	$1,025	

Now the numbers are clear. If we put down $12,000, we'll come out $88 ahead at the end of the year, after taxes. If we put down no money, the property will cost us $775 a year in negative cash flow after taxes, or 6.5 percent of $12,000. This means that 6.5 percent is the effective rate we are paying to borrow that $12,000 from the seller.

Unless you know somewhere else where you can borrow money for even less, or unless you have cash coming out of your ears, this is a pretty good deal. If we can't make more than 6.5 percent by using that money elsewhere, then we don't belong in the real estate business.

You'll find that as your investing grows, the one or two houses you've purchased can be snow-balled into a sizable estate. The houses you bought at wholesale prices can be sold for good profits. What's more, as rents increase, so will your cash flow. Before long, you'll be operating at such a profit that you won't mind paying a few dollars of taxes on your annual gains.

REAL LOSSES

Up until now we've talked mostly about paper losses, the tax benefits of depreciation. Of course, negative cash flow isn't a paper loss. It comes right out of your pocket. But unfortunately, it isn't the only expense that does. Maintenance costs can be all too real. The fact that they come out of your money hurts, but it will hurt you even more if you don't take full advantage of the tax breaks.

Employ Others, Not Yourself

Do you like working for yourself? Not on your own properties, you don't, unless you already have more than enough tax shelter. If you do your own labor, you are working for free, not for yourself, but for Uncle Sam. It's great to be a patriot, but do you really want to carry it that far?

The IRS doesn't let you deduct your own labor. As far as they're concerned, you're a tax volunteer. But if you hire someone to work on your property while you work on something else, that's tax-deductible. You're hiring someone to work in your business, so whatever you pay them is a business expense.

But you must keep accurate records. If they're employees, you must pay withholding tax and Social Security tax as well as any state or local payroll taxes. And you have to keep records on all of that.

This is why you don't want employees. You want to work with independent contractors. They're responsible for keeping their own records and paying their own taxes. Instead of keeping people on salary, you hire and pay them by the job. This is simple, inexpensive, and keeps everyone honest. As we've mentioned before, our handyman is an independent businessman. We may be his most important customers, but we aren't his employers. This leads to many advantages. It cuts down our record-keeping, and it also ensures that he will do a good job. If he doesn't, we don't have to fire him. We just don't use him anymore. It's much simpler and cleaner that way.

Repairs, Not Improvements

Another important factor to remember is that repairs can be deducted in the year they're made, while improvements have to be *amortized*. Therefore, you get more tax write-offs for repairs than for improvements. Since it's a fine line between them, the difference between improvements and repairs is often a matter of the way you write them up. If you remodel the kitchen and/ or bathroom, are you improving the property for the purpose of increasing the value, or are you making necessary repairs? It never hurts to make notations on the back of all bills, stating exactly what they are for.

Tax-Deductible Management

If you pay someone else to manage your property, you can deduct that. If you manage your own houses, you can deduct the costs of maintaining an office for your rental property, trips to and from your property, and related expenses. You can deduct all this even if owning rental property isn't your primary business. As long as you own the property for the primary purpose of renting it and making money on it, you can deduct all your business expenses that are connected with that property. If you keep good records, you should have quite a few deductions by the end of the year.

MORE SHELTER

If you start running short of tax shelter, there's usually an easy solution. Either you need to buy more houses, or you need to refinance the ones you've got. Sometimes you need to do both. Refinancing can give you tax-free cash to buy more houses with. It can also give you more tax write-off by creating higher interest payments. The tax-free cash you get should more than help you offset the cost of these payments, and you'll be getting extra tax write-off besides.

As long as you can afford the payments, it's never a bad idea to turn equity into cash anyway. That way, if anything ever happens to the economy and property values go down, you'll have most of your money out of the property. If the economy is good and property values go up, you still have control of the property and benefit from the appreciation. You aren't hit with the tax consequences of a sale.

On the other hand, because you don't want to make your payments uncomfortably high, refinancing isn't an automatic panacea for every situation. Any time you plan your investment strategy around taxes, you'll have problems. You should plan your investment first, setting your goals to get the maximum return. Then figure in the tax angle and see how it really works out, which investment gives you the best tax return on your money. If you do this conscientiously over a period of time, it will bring you to our next chapter, "Tracking Your Properties."

Fifteen

Tracking Your Properties

When we talk about tracking our houses, we don't mean that we have to get out the bloodhounds and hunt down properties that have run off and disappeared. We mean that we keep records on each house to see which ones are the most profitable for us, and why.

We firmly believe in holding properties for long-term investments and positive cash flow. Our whole program and this whole book are based on that idea. But we don't believe in holding on to any house at any cost. Some houses aren't worth holding, so we get rid of them.

We heard a man speak at a real estate conference, and he advocated the idea of buying real estate only for recycling—turning it over for a profit as quickly as possible. He was totally against the idea of holding on to long-term rental properties. His position was a bit extreme. We believe that people should do whatever feels comfortable. Some people can handle all the pressures and responsibility of being a landlord, others can't, but his ideas still made a lot of sense.

His basic premise was that too many people buy real estate without thinking carefully. They get stuck on the idea of becoming rich simply by buying and owning a lot of real estate. Many of them then hang on to their real estate through thick, thin, and negative cash flow when they could actually get a better return on their money by investing it in something else.

This is why it's necessary to track your properties. How do you know where you're going if you don't know where you've been? A very successful businessman once said that he preferred losing money and knowing why he lost it to making money without knowing why. Again, this is an extreme view, but the basic proposition makes sense. If you're making money but don't know how or why, then you aren't in control of your business and that isn't a healthy situation. It's just a matter of time before things get out of control and you start losing, and losing big.

BUYING THE FUTURE

We start tracking our houses before we buy them. We have to know all about the area and its history before we look at a house. Otherwise, we're wasting our time and the seller's time. We aren't overly concerned about the seller's time, but we do care about our own. It's valuable, so why should we fool around looking at houses we don't intend to buy?

If a neighborhood has a bad history or just isn't a good rental area, for whatever reason, then it doesn't matter how nice the house is. If the area has a high vacancy rate, or a lot of transients or undesirables live there, we look somewhere else. This is the main cornerstone of our "buy right to manage right" philosophy.

Some areas are bad, period. Those are usually easy to spot, and you stay away from them. After all, why knowingly buy anything in a bad area? The real problem is with the more subtle, borderline areas. These are the ones that don't necessarily seem bad, but do attract a lot of transient people. If a neighborhood has that sort of reputation, then that's whom it's going to attract: people on the move.

Again, neighborhoods change, and sometimes an area will start off stable but gradually change after you already own property there. Be on the lookout for changing conditions and be ready to respond to them. For example, if an area is full of elderly people who have lived there for years, you know changes are due soon. Stability can turn to quick and frequent turnovers almost overnight as longtime residents start to die off or retire and move away. In many cases where there are good schools or attractive houses, this leads to a general upgrading of the area as the older residents are replaced by upwardly mobile young professionals who have more money to put into maintaining their properties and improving them. But often the area will go the other way. The homes are taken over by people who don't have the money or the interest to maintain them properly, or to repair any deterioration. When slumlords move in, for example, formerly stable neighborhoods can rapidly destabilize.

For the same reason, we try to stay away from neighborhoods where most of the occupants are renters. Not all landlords are as careful about whom they rent to as we are, and a lot of lifetime tenants don't behave very responsibly. All it takes is one or two of the irresponsible ones to move in on a street. They seem to be able to turn a neat, clean property into a weed-infested junkyard overnight—a night that's made miserable for the neighbors by the rowdy housewarming the new tenants throw to thank all the friends who helped put those rusty old cars up on blocks in the frontyard.

When this happens, the good tenants in the area start moving out faster than you can say "thirty-day notice." After all, they don't have any equity to protect by calling the police or notifying the owner that he'd better do something before everyone's property values are destroyed. It's much easier to move to a better neighborhood than try to maintain one that's going downhill, especially when it isn't really your problem.

That's why we look for houses in neighborhoods that are largely owner-occupied. People who own their homes usually take better care of them, and they're concerned about the rest of their neighborhood, too. If someone's tenant steps out of line —including one of ours—nearby home owners will usually notify the landlord pretty quickly. This suits us just fine, since if it is one of our tenants, it alerts us to a problem so we can handle it before it goes too far. If it's not our tenant, of course, that's even better. It's some other landlord's job to straighten out the guilty party or get rid of him. This natural interest the owner-occupants have in keeping up neighborhood standards not only makes our job easier, but also helps keep up the value of our property.

On the other hand, we've occasionally found that some areas

are just too nice, and they attract people who are overqualified to be renters. These people are the ones who end up buying their own homes. If we find that we're getting too many of these people in some of our homes, we stop buying in those areas. We'll even consider getting rid of the houses we already have in that neighborhood if the turnover is too frequent and too regular.

We remain aware, too, that areas change over the years. Ideally, they change for the better, but unfortunately, this isn't always the case. Go to any major city and you'll find that hardly any of the run-down slum areas were designed as housing for the poor. Most of them were originally middle- and upper-class neighborhoods that simply ran down with age.

Many property owners—residents and investors alike—got caught when those areas changed. Some people saw the changes coming and got out in time, but many others didn't and they lived to regret their mistakes. We never intend to let anything like that happen to us. We keep track of what happens to our neighborhoods. Most of them are improving, so our properties are going up in value. But occasionally we make a mistake, or things begin to change after we've bought the property, and we have to dispose of a house before it becomes a liability. We aren't in business to support our real estate. In the long run, we expect our real estate to support us.

WATCH YOUR HOUSES CAREFULLY

Our houses give us very little aggravation, particularly the ones we hold on to. We try to buy in areas that generally have a low vacancy rate to begin with, and then we monitor our own turnover carefully. Ideally, our houses stay rented to the same people for years. Once we get the tenants, we do all we can to hold on to them, because stability makes our business work.

Some turnovers are inevitable, but if we start getting too many, we sit down to figure out what's going wrong. Sometimes it's something we were doing wrong, especially when we were first getting started. But other times, it turns out to be the area that's driving our tenants away. We watch our houses carefully to keep this from happening to us. We drive by them periodically to see what they look like and how they're being maintained. We keep in touch with the neighbors, and we stay alert for any developments that might affect our property.

Is a new freeway being built somewhere in town? How is that likely to affect us? We want to know. Is it going to make the neighborhoods where we own property more accessible? Is it going to create jobs and bring people into the area? Or is it going to drive them away? Will the noise and pollution make the neighborhood less attractive? Will there be a "right" side of the freeway and a "wrong" side? If so, which side is our property likely to be on?

What are the employment prospects in the area? This is getting to be *the* question for the '80s. If people can't find steady work, how can they possibly be stable, steady tenants? Sure, people will commute, but most of them would rather not unless they have a really good reason. If jobs are leaving the area, we want to leave with them. We don't want to wake up someday and find ourselves stuck in a ghost town or a run-down area that used to be nice.

Listen to Tenants

We also keep a close check on the rental of the individual houses we have within any area. If one or two houses have a constant turnover, while five or six others don't, we know the problem isn't the area. We also know that it isn't us. By now, our system is functioning pretty smoothly, and we know that it works most of the time. So we figure that something must be wrong with the house itself or with the specific location.

Maybe the neighbors are the problem. We've been hit with everything from simple loud parties to whole families of thieves and burglars living right next door. There are all sorts of problems that even the smartest, most experienced investor can't predict in advance. The best you can do is keep your ear to the ground. Listen to the rumblings from your tenants. You don't want to be married to them, but you don't want to lose touch, either. You must reach and maintain a balance. If you have good stable tenants, don't ignore them. They obviously require less supervision than problem tenants, but that doesn't mean that you should forget about them

Keep in touch with them. Make sure they're still satisfied, and then find out why. What are you doing right that you can put into practice with your other properties? We like to think that we learn a lot more from our own successes than we do from our mistakes, simply because we have so many successes to learn from, and it's more fun. It's a positive learning experience, instead of a negative experience. That helps give us the energy to go on, as well as giving us new ideas.

It also helps us ward off a vacancy problem we never even anticipated. Every time interest rates take a dip, we find we lose some of our best tenants. They aren't unhappy or dissatisfied. They just want to buy homes of their own. We're victims of our high standards. Instead of getting ordinary renters, we get many would-be home owners. Most of them never intended to rent for any longer than necessary.

That's a problem for us, of course, but at least it's not because we are doing something wrong or because a particular house or neighborhood has a major defect. Our buying methods and careful ownership usually keep us from running into those situations. Occasionally, though, we find ourselves with a house that we simply can't keep good tenants in, and then we have to do something about it.

Cut Your Losses

If a house isn't performing up to our expectations, we have to get rid of it. We have no more time to deal with problem houses than we have to deal with problem tenants. We're in an active, constantly changing business, and the dead wood just has to go. This is the second reason, besides taxes, why we like to keep good records. We want to know a lot of things about our properties: how much they have gone up in value since we bought them, how much income they bring in, how much it costs to maintain them, what the vacancy rate is.

It's only when we have all this information that we can begin to cross-reference it, analyze everything, and then decide how to proceed. Just looking at the appreciation rate or the vacancy factor alone won't do it. Many different factors go into the decision about how long to hold a property and when and how to dispose of it. Economic returns have to be balanced against the time involved in running a property and the emotional toll it takes. A lot of people make a lot of money with ghetto properties, for example, but we don't, because we don't want to put up with the aggravation.

We want stability. We want long-term tenants who know that owning a home is not for them. These are the people who pay the bills, month in and year out. They're the glue that holds our business together. Without them, it might not exactly come apart, but it would be a lot more difficult to maintain. But, of course, the one thing worse than instability is the problem of vacancies. We can even live with a relatively high turnover rate, as long as it's always easy to rerent the property.

The one thing we can't afford is a property that's hard to rent. We're in business. We need income to keep our business going. If a house has a turnover problem, but rents easily each time, we can get by without losing money. It will mean more work, but we might even be able to raise the rent more often, knowing that the tenants will probably be transient anyway.

But if the old tenant leaves and we haven't got a new tenant lined up, we lose money. There are no two ways about it. Turnover or not, we have got to keep most of our houses rented all the time or we will go under. Therefore, we watch the vacancy rate carefully—very carefully. And we also look closely at what causes each vacancy. For instance, evictions haven't been a problem for us. But if we ever get a second eviction at one of our houses, we will be very cautious. A third eviction in one house would mean it was definitely time to sell that property.

That's the nice thing about single-family homes. You have a liquidity. If you have a problem property, you can usually unload it, and it may not even be a problem for the next owner. A house may not make a good rental, but it could be perfect for a home owner—or at least good enough, especially under the right terms and conditions.

FIVE-YEAR PLAN

Our overall game plan is to keep each of our houses for at least five years. We believe in inflation. We believe that it will inevitably drive up prices and rents, so that our income and our net worth will both grow. Five years should be long enough for most properties to weather most cycles. Real estate doesn't go up or down in value in nice, neat, vertical lines. It reaches a plateau where prices level off and maybe even decline a bit, and then after a year or two, prices usually start going up again.

The important thing is flexibility. The ideal time to sell may be in three years instead of five, if we think prices are about to peak. Or it may not be for six or seven years if we are in an economic slump. We aren't fortune tellers. If we were, we would have no need to worry about keeping records, except for tax purposes. We wouldn't have to worry about a property's past performance, and we would know the future.

Wouldn't that be nice? Too bad it's just a fantasy. We don't know the future except by studying the past and then hoping for the best, keeping our eyes open and trying to stay ahead of the many changes happening all around us all the time. That's why we track our properties, and why you should track yours. With practice, you'll get pretty good at it. It will help you the entire time you're building and managing your real estate empire. Even better, you'll find that it improves your return when you're ready to retire.

Sixteen

Putting It on Automatic Pilot

If you feel you've put in all the time you want to put in as a landlord and now you're ready to sit back and reap your reward, then this chapter is for you. If you think paper is fine for decorating walls, but it's not something you put much faith in as payment for all your efforts, then read on. The sad truth is that cashing out appeals to sellers more then it does to buyers. In fact, buyers usually have a distinct preference for sellers who are willing to carry paper.

GOOD CASH BUYERS ARE HARD TO FIND

Of course, many of these people aren't the ones you want to attract anyway. You want buyers who will fall in love with the property and not worry about the financing, since those are the buyers who will pay top dollar. You can't expect to find these people on every streetcorner, though. You'll have to go out and look for them. If you're determined to cash out, you have your work cut out for you. You'll have to come up with dynamic, exciting, enticing ads, and then wait for a response.

You'll also have to decide what to do if offers come in asking you to carry some paper. If you turn them down, the buyers *may* come back with all-cash offers—or they may not come back at all. Are you prepared for this kind of psychological letdown? Rejection hurts, even if you've brought it on yourself.

Not every buyer is going to like your property anyway. But if you insist on cash, you'll cut down the number of potentially serious buyers even further.

In other words, unless you're in an extraordinarily hot seller's market, you can forget about making a quick sale if you insist on all cash. The other side of the coin is that you can forget about selling for all cash if you need a quick sale. The two ideas simply do not go together. If you want cash, be prepared to sit on your property—and sit, and sit, and sit.

Of course, viable alternatives exist, and you should be aware of and consider them. You *can* sell your property and get your cash, too. Here are some simple methods to help you do this.

REFINANCING

Refinancing works well if you have a good income, good credit, and some equity in the property. You simply refinance the first loan, or get a new second or third loan just before you sell the property. You keep the proceeds, and the buyer picks up the monthly payments.

Of course, the buyer has to be willing to take over the payments. If the interest rate on the new loan is too high, that could make the property hard to sell. On the other hand, the buyer doesn't have to do anything to get you your cash, since you've already gotten it before the buyer entered the picture. If you refinance, the buyer doesn't have to come up with much down payment money, either. He or she must take over your monthly payments instead. It's all very easy, as long as the new loan you get is assumable. That's an absolute necessity.

SELLING PAPER

Carrying back some paper and then selling it for cash is another possibility. There's a flourishing market in notes, and people buy and sell them every day. The only problem is that notes always sell at a discount. No one wants to pay face value for them. This means that you must either get the buyer to pay more for the property, or you must accept the fact that your net will be lower.

For example, let's say you want to sell a house for $80,000, and it has a $50,000 assumable loan. This leaves you with $30,000 equity. You'd like to cash out, but that doesn't seem possible. The property has been on the market for several months, and you've given up hoping for an all-cash offer. Finally, you accept an offer with $10,000 down and a note for $20,000 at 12 percent per annum, interest-only payments for five years. You then turn around to sell the note, and find that you can get only $13,000 cash for your $20,000 note. This means you really accepted $73,000 for your property instead of $80,000.

As an alternative to losing $7,000, you could accept $10,000 down and a note for $30,000. Then you could sell your $30,000 note for $20,000 to get your full $80,000 asking price and receive your entire $30,000 equity in cash. An even better alternative is to carry two notes for $15,000 each, or one for $20,000 and one for $10,000. Smaller notes are easier to sell.

However you do it, cashing out will require work and patience. In the end, you may have to accept less money than you hoped to get, and you may have to limit the number of properties you put on the market at any one time, although at least you'll get your money. You won't have to worry about the buyer defaulting, or getting the property back, or any of the other pitfalls of carrying paper. Chances are, though, that the day will come when you at least consider carrying a note on property you're selling. In fact, it's likely that if you sell several properties, there will be at least one or two you'll have to carry paper on to close the deal. When that time comes, we want you to be able to do it as profitably as you can, so let's look at some carryback opportunities.

Why Carry Paper?

As usual, we've exaggerated to point up what some people imagine could happen. Most people who want you to carry paper when they purchase your property are honest and well-meaning, so while you should always check out your buyers carefully, carrying paper is a decision you should give careful thought to.

There are many obvious advantages—for one thing, it makes the property more appealing to a wide range of buyers. There are also potential problems, so if you're short on cash, you should probably insist on cashing out and take what you can get. If you carry paper and the buyer defaults, you may be unable to protect yourself, so you might lose out and get nothing.

But before we dwell on the possible trouble spots, let's look at the advantages of carrying paper and the reasons why you shouldn't automatically rule it out. First of all, it opens up your possibilities. Many buyers who would be scared away if you demanded all cash will respond positively to the suggestion that you might carry all or part of the loan. Everyone prefers dealing with someone who is flexible, and the more offers you get, the more chances you have to get one you like.

Secondly, carrying paper offers you a chance to earn interest. No one expects you to carry paper for free. Often you get a much better return then you could by taking cash and putting it in the bank. If you have something definite to spend the money on, that's one thing. But if you don't, carrying paper can be a good money-making investment. In fact, a good way to increase your equity's money-making potential is to use the wraparound (also known as the all-inclusive, or overriding, deed of trust or mortgage). This handy technique allows you to play banker and make money on someone else's money. You'll borrow low and lend high.

It works like this: You're selling your house for $80,000. It has a $50,000 assumable loan, and you're going to get $10,000 cash from the buyer and carry a note for $20,000. Well, the wraparound is a better way to handle this. Instead of passing that $50,000 loan on to the buyer and then carrying a second for $20,000, you carry an all-inclusive mortgage or deed of trust for $70,000.

This way you're in first position, not second. If the buyer defaults, you don't have to worry about paying off any senior liens before you can foreclose. This is one big advantage of using a wraparound. Another advantage is money. You can make more of it by using a wraparound because you make money on the lender's money.

For example, let's say that the existing $50,000 loan is at 9 percent interest with payments of $402.32 a month. You offer the buyer a $70,000 wraparound at 12 percent, and he pays you $720.03 a month. You pocket the difference: $317 a month profit. You make 12 percent on your own $20,000 and 3 percent interest on the original lender's $50,000.

There are other ways to profit from carrying paper. We've already talked about selling the notes you carry, but you can also borrow against them if you don't want to sell them. This is known as hypothecating notes, which is a fancy way of saying you're putting them up as collateral for loans. This way the money you get is tax-free, and you still get to keep the notes, although you probably won't be able to borrow more than about 70 percent of their face value. But it's nice to know that you don't have to pay taxes on that money.

Even if you do have to pay some taxes, you'll pay less if you carry some paper. The sale can then be considered an install-ment sale, and you pay taxes only on the amount of money that you actually receive each year instead of on your entire gain all at once. This can be an excellent way to maximize the benefits of owning real estate by keeping more of your hard-earned prof-its for yourself. After all, Uncle Sam didn't share in all the work, so why should you give him any more of the rewards than you absolutely have to?

A WORD OF CAUTION

Of course, you don't want to get so overzealous about shielding your profits that you wind up throwing them away altogether. Always remember that carrying paper does entail risks. It's never quite as safe as cashing out and knowing that your in-volvement with the property is completely over and that the new owner can burn it down for all you care. When you agree to carry paper, you're never completely free of the property until the note is paid off. Until then, it's still your responsibility, and you could be the ultimate loser if anything goes wrong. If the buyer stops making his payments, can you afford to foreclose and then make up those back payments to keep the property from going into default? If your answer is no, you should think seriously about holding out for all cash.

But if you're not really cash poor and you feel that you're in a good position to protect your interests if need be, carrying paper—especially on a wraparound where you're in first position—can give you all the rewards of being a landlord (e.g., a nice steady income each and every month) without having to put up with any more tenants. Properly used, it can be one of the ultimate steps in your quest for financial freedom.

You can also hold on to your property and reap many of the rewards of ownership without the responsibilities. In the beginning, of course, you are going to have to exert some real effort as a landlord. But once your program is successfully launched and running, you should be able to stand back from it and eventually let it run itself. Ultimately, you should be able to step back completely and just watch the money roll in. That is the ultimate goal of landlording, to create a perpetual money machine that goes on producing cash long after you stop cranking the handle.

Most people assume they will sell their properties someday and get cash. Others assume they will keep trading up until they die, so they will never have to pay taxes, but these are not the only—or always the best—alternatives. There are several different ways to sell your property and still have income coming in or even retain a piece of the future appreciation.

Sometimes cashing out is best. Other times, trading up is the answer. But you have to be aware of all the choices before you can intelligently make a decision.

CREATIVE FINANCING IS NOT JUST FOR BUYERS

Creative financing works for sellers as well. True creativity helps everyone. Don't just sell your property. Figure out what you want and need and then go ahead and market it, instead. Decide on the best way to get the most from your equity and build your marketing plan around that idea and make the buyer think that it's benefiting him.

Carry back your equity in a note instead of cashing out. This

way, you can get an ongoing income long after the property is off
your hands. Don't ask for all cash just because that's what
you've always been told to do. Think carefully about your own
situation and ask yourself if that's really the best thing for you.
Do you have a real need or even an immediate use for a substantial amount of cash? What are you really going to do with it?

A good deal of the time, people don't really have an answer
to this question. They don't have a definite purpose in mind.
They just want the cash, because that's what's real to them.
That's the tangible reward for selling the property. Getting a
note just doesn't seem the same. This is an emotional response,
not a logical one. The logical thing to do is sit down and work
out the numbers. Figure out what you're going to do with the
cash and how much you expect to earn. Then compare that to
the return you will get by carrying a note and then see which
one works out better.

Remember to add in all the variables, such as the fact that you
might get a higher price by carrying a note, you might get the
property sold faster, and you should save on taxes, besides.
There is no point to comparing the returns you will get before
taxes, unless you have all your income sheltered in other ways.
What you really want to compare is the net return, what you
will get after taxes. This is what really matters.

For example, let's say you originally paid $50,000 for the
property and now you're selling it for $100,000. That gives you
a gross gain of $100,000, but you've also been depreciating the
property. You've taken $2,000 a year worth of depreciation
write-offs for the last five years, so that lowers your basis in the
property to $40,000 and boosts your gross profit to $60,000. But
you've also had $20,000 in deductible expenses in connection
with fixing up the property and preparing it for sale, so this
means your net gain is $40,000. This $40,000 is the amount that
gets added to your taxable income for that year. If you are in
the 28 percent tax bracket, then this will cost you $11,200 out of
your $40,000 profit.

If you carry a note instead, you can minimize the tax bite.
Although you pay tax on 100 percent of the profit you collect on
the note, you pay tax only on the amount of principal and interest that you actually collect in any given year. So if you take

only $10,000 in principal and interest the first year, for instance, the most you would have to pay in tax would be $2,800 (assuming your tax bracket is 28%.)

You have to take all that into account, when you decide whether to cash out or carry a note.

Imputed Interest

This is something else you have to think about when you carry a note. Many people consider it a problem, but actually, if you put it in the proper perspective, the IRS is doing sellers a favor by forcing them to charge a relatively high rate of interest. Everyone's got to charge the same interest rate. It's the law. If sellers don't charge an interest rate equal to at least 9 percent then the IRS will impute an interest rate of 10 percent. The seller will be taxed on this basis, just as if he had actually received all that interest as income. People selling their own homes for less than $250,000 are exempt from this rule.

Some people say this will kill owner financing, but we say it will just make it more profitable for sellers. It will eliminate competition among sellers. With no one offering low interest rates, because of the new imputed interest rule, buyers will no longer be able to play one seller against the other.

Buyers will still appreciate owner-assisted financing, even if it doesn't mean lower interest rates for them. There is still the advantage of flexibility. Sellers are not usually as rigid about qualifying buyers as institutional lenders are. They are more likely to deal with people as individuals.

Owner financing can still help buyers to get into the property with little or no money down. Particularly when the existing financing is assumable, or the property is free and clear, owner financing—even at high interest rates—can help make the property affordable for buyers without money.

The minimum interest rates mandated by the new tax law are designed to be higher than the interest rate a seller could get by putting his money into Treasury bills, certificates of deposit, or money market accounts. This is designed to discourage buyers from relying on owner financing, but it should encourage sellers to offer owner financing because of the increased profits they will make.

You've got to choose your buyers carefully, even more carefully than you pick your tenants, but think of how nice it could be to have that ongoing income. Instead of taking your profit in one lump sum and not really knowing what to do with it anyway, you spread the payments out over five years and then add 13 percent to 15 percent per year. You can reap benefits long after the property is gone.

LEASE OPTIONS

Lease options are a way to put your properties on automatic pilot without relinquishing total control. You retain title to the property until the option is exercised. You remain in control and you get all the tax benefits of owning the property, but the tenants take care of the maintenance. After all, they are going to buy the property, aren't they? So naturally they are going to take care of it.

You don't want to give away any free equity or future appreciation, but there are a couple of ways of covering yourself so you can avoid this. You can set the option price deliberately high to allow for inflation, or you can leave it open, to be determined by an independent appraiser at the actual time of sale.

The Option Fee

Charge an option fee, since you are giving the tenants a privilege by granting them an option to buy the property. This is standard procedure. The fee can be anywhere from $50 to a few thousand dollars and it's not taxable until the option is either exercised or expires.

This is one easy way to compensate yourself for having your property tied up. You get your cash now and you don't get taxed on it until later. If the tenant decides not to exercise the option, you keep the option fee anyway. Either way, you come out ahead.

The Increased Rent-Lease Option

Raise the rent during the option period and get the tenants to pay for the option that way. Most people will pay more rent for a place they have an option to buy. If they really like the place and the rent increase is not too outrageous, then what are they going to do? Move?

If necessary, you can credit the increased rent toward the purchase price if the tenants decide to exercise the option. This gives them an incentive to pay the extra money—and to exercise the option. If they don't exercise the option, then you have gotten extra money each month anyway, so how can you go wrong?

You can go wrong if the tenant takes you to court. He may try to claim that the portion of the option fee or the monthly rent that was to be credited toward the purchase price, constitutes equity in the property. This has happened to more than one hapless seller, but it can easily be avoided.

You must state clearly in both the lease and the option agreement that any portion of the rent or the option fee that is to be credited toward the purchase price does *not* constitute equity that the tenant/buyer is accumulating in the property. It is a bonus to be automatically forfeited if the tenant-buyer does not exercise the option and purchase the property within the option period.

The beauty of lease options is that they can be set up so you win either way, whether you're buying or selling. In fact, you can even make money by lowering your rent and then offering to lease-option the property. Almost anything can work to your advantage if you're truly creative.

The Decreased Rent-Lease Option

Give tenants a lease option at below-market rents. This may sound strange, but it can and does work. In some areas, rent-control laws will prevent you from raising the rent, even if you offer tenants an option to buy the property. There will be a maximum legal rent set for the area and no way you can get around it legally.

In other areas, the law of the marketplace, the law of supply and demand will prevent you from getting the rents you want. You will find that no one will pay the rent you are asking just for an option to buy the property.

In either of these cases, the decreased rent-lease option can be the solution. You attract tenant-buyers with the low rent and the idea of the lease option and then you get your money back by charging them a high option fee and setting the option price high, as well. That way, you make money whether they exercise the option and buy the property or not.

For example, on a one-year lease option, you might lower the rent by $100 a month, or $1,200 for the year and then charge a $3,000 to $5,000 option fee. As long as the option price is set high enough to allow for appreciation and inflation, you have to come out ahead. You get your cash up front and an additional profit if the option is exercised. If the option is not exercised, you start all over again.

LIMITED PARTNERSHIPS

Limited partnerships offer unlimited opportunities. The best partnerships are based on positive cash flow with less emphasis on tax shelter. You can set them up so that most of the tax benefits can be used to shelter all or part of the positive cash flow the property generates.

By contacting tax advisers, accountants, and other qualified professionals, you can find people who need cash flow that is sheltered from taxation. You then can sell them shares in your limited partnership and retain a piece of the action for yourself. Then as the general partner, you can hire a management company to handle the day-to-day running of the properties while you sit back and cruise through your early and luxurious retirement as the automatic pilot keeps your income right on course and steers you right toward our next chapter, "Equity Sharing: A Management Tool for the '80s and Beyond."

Seventeen

Equity Sharing: A Management Tool for the '80s and Beyond

Equity sharing can help reduce, if not eliminate, your management problems and help make your properties more profitable at the same time. Equity sharing works a lot the way lease options work. By giving the tenant a stake in the property, by making him feel as though he is a home owner, that he has something to lose, and more important, something to gain, you give him a reason to cooperate. You give him a reason to care what happens to the property. You give him a reason for wanting to see that the property runs smoothly.

OWNER OCCUPANTS MAKE BETTER TENANTS

If a tenant feels he is going to own the property someday, he is not going to cause problems. He is going to stay on your good side. He is going to pay his rent on time. He is going to keep the property in good shape. If he trashes it, he will be trashing his own investment. He is going to be a trouble-free tenant, the kind of tenant you want to deal with.

The problem is, lease options don't always work. In some situations they won't work for you because you don't really want to sell the property. You may find you just can't seem to get people to pay enough rent to cover your payments unless you offer them an option on really reasonable terms. And if you do offer prospective tenants an option at reasonable terms, the chances are they are going to take you up on it. They are going to exercise their option to purchase the property and you will wind up having to sell it, whether you want to or not.

In other cases you are going to find that a lease option just isn't attractive enough to prospective tenants, no matter how reasonable the terms are. If you are in a strong tenant's market or a strong buyer's market, you might find that the prospect of a lease option just doesn't excite people—particularly if they will have to come up with down-payment money and/or qualify for a loan in order to exercise the option and purchase the property.

In order to bring in enough rent to cover your payments, you may have to try some other alternatives. You may have to find some other way of convincing tenants that they have a stake in the property. Equity sharing can be an excellent way to do this. It can work with properties you already own as well as with properties you are contemplating buying. There are three basic ways you can use it.

THREE WAYS TO USE EQUITY SHARING

You can share your equity with a tenant. This is probably the most common form of equity sharing. You can share ownership with the tenant who is already in the property, or you can advertise for a tenant who wants to be half owner of a property and is willing to take on some extra responsibility.

Many people don't like the idea of dealing with tenants as home buyers and partners. It makes them nervous. They feel that tenants should be treated as tenants and that giving them a share in the property just confuses the relationship and creates problems.

If you feel this way, then one of your alternatives is to share equity with a home buyer instead. Find someone who wants to purchase their own home but who can't qualify for a loan at today's interest rates. Or find someone who can't come up with the down payment required to purchase a home today. Offer him a chance to own half of your property with little or no money down in exchange for making the monthly payments.

Of course, it's a thin line between a home buyer and a tenant. The key factor is attitude. A tenant is somebody who thinks of himself as a renter, a nonowner. A home buyer is someone who thinks of himself as a home owner, not a renter, even though he hasn't been able to buy a home yet. A home buyer has a different attitude toward property and so he should take better care of it. But there are never any guarantees.

Fortunately, for those of you who feel that a tenant by any other name is still a tenant and don't feel comfortable putting someone on title and having them live in your property unless they are going to put up some down-payment money, there is one more alternative available. You can share some of the equity in the proprerty with another investor. You can find someone who is willing to make up the gap between the normal rent you would get from a tenant and the amount of rent you need to cover your monthly payments. This way, you wouldn't have the problem of having someone living in your property, paying rent, and calling himself half owner of the property. If you get into any disputes with your nonresident partner, you won't have to worry about evicting him. And you won't have to worry about making the entire payment on your own, because you will have the property rented.

So those are your three choices. You can go for a tenant, preferably the tenant who is already in the property, or another tenant if necessary. You can go for a would-be home buyer who can't afford to buy a home on his own. Or you can find an investor who doesn't want to live in the property but wants to help make those payments in exchange for a share of the ownership and a share of the tax benefits the property generates.

APPEALING TO EXISTING TENANTS

How do you go about attracting these co-owners? It's very simple. First, you approach the tenant who is in the property and you offer him a deal. For example, if you have a property where your payments are $800 a month and the normal rent is $600 a month, you just contact the tenant and say, "Look, you have been a good tenant. How would you like to be part owner of the property? By paying $600 a month all you are getting is the right to live here. You are never going to get any equity in the property. You are never going to get any of the benefits of ownership. You are not going to get any appreciation. It is not going to be doing anything for your credit rating or your standing in the world and you are not going to be getting any of the tax benefits that you would get from owning real estate. Wouldn't you much rather be an owner?''

The chances are, if you have a good tenant—the kind of tenant you want, the responsible type of family-oriented tenant you should have put in the property in the first place—he is going to say, "Sure. Of course I would rather be a home owner. But the problem is I can't afford to be a home owner. I can't qualify for a loan at today's prices and I can't come up with the down-payment money to buy a home.''

In that case you can just make the tenant a simple offer. You say, "Look, Mr. Tenant. I have a problem and you have a problem. I have a property and I can't meet the payments. Your rent is only $600 a month. My payments are $800 a month. You would like to buy a house but you say you can't afford to. So I have a solution. Why don't we each solve each others' problem? I will give you half of this house and make you co-owner, eligible for half the appreciation and half the tax write-offs if you will just make the entire payment. This means that instead of paying $600 a month, you will pay $800 a month. It will cost you an extra $200 a month out of your pocket. But in return for that $200 a month you are going to get half ownership in the property and you are going to get all the benefits of half ownership including half of the tax write-offs.

"Instead of paying rent and not getting anything for it, you get a tax write-off. Instead of paying rent you are going to be making house payments, and 99 percent of those house payments will be interest, and interest is tax deductible. Another portion of that house payment is going to go to property taxes and property taxes are also tax deductible, so you are actually going to be saving money.

"Chances are, you will wind up not taking any money at all out of your pocket. By the time you figure in the tax savings, you may even come out ahead. And think of the appreciation you are going to be getting. Five years from now or ten years from now, you will be glad you did it because you will be a property owner. If you go on renting you will save two hundred dollars a month, but five years from now, ten years from now, twenty years from now, you will still be a tenant and you will have no more interest in the property than you have today. You will have not built up equity. You will have no tax benefits. Is that really what you want to do with your money? Wouldn't you rather build up a stake for the future?''

Assuming you have the right kind of tenant, he is probably going to jump at this chance. Just the fact that you are giving him a chance to get part ownership of the property without putting up a down payment is a great deal. Then, when you throw in the fact that he doesn't even have to qualify, he doesn't have to go to the bank and get the loan and jump through all the hoops; he doesn't have to come up with verification of employment and verification of deposit, verification of where his down-payment money is coming from, he can deal with you, a real live human being instead of a bank bureaucracy, this just makes it even better.

ADVERTISING FOR EQUITY-SHARE TENANTS

But let's say that for one reason or another, your tenant doesn't go for this. Maybe you made a mistake and he really is not the type of ambitious, family-oriented person you thought he was. Or maybe he just really can't afford the extra $200 a month. Maybe his money situation is just that bad. Or maybe he is saving his money in order to buy another property outright. Whatever the reason, you can't come to an agreement with the tenant who is in there, so your next step is to advertise. Put an ad in the "Homes for Rent" column; an ad like the following:

> Why rent when you can own? Call today. Be a home owner tomorrow. No money down. No qualifying. Half ownership in fine property—$800 a month. Call . . .

Get yourself an answering machine or an answering service. Be prepared: the phone is going to be ringing off the hook. You are going to have more calls than you know what to do with, and your big problem will be sorting through them and finding the right candidate. If you thought you had to give tenants a thorough interview before you rented to them, think about how carefully you have to interview a potential co-owner. Now you are going to be putting somebody on title. You are going to be sharing your property with someone. You are giving him the right to call himself co-owner. You want to be even more careful about whom you are dealing with. You want to check him out even more carefully. You want to interview him even more thoroughly.

ADVERTISING FOR EQUITY-SHARE HOME BUYERS

The first step is to get those phone calls. If you don't feel comfortable sharing equity in your property with tenants, then instead of putting an ad in the "Homes to Rent" column, put it in the "Homes for Sale" column. This is how you attract prospective home buyers.

You word your ad a little bit differently. These people have already decided that they want to own rather than rent and so you don't even have to mention it. Just say something like,

> Own a home. No money down. No qualifying. Half
> interest for sale—$800 a month.

It is simple, to the point, and it should grab people's attention. Needless to say, you want to save for last the fact that you're offering only a half interest. You want to grab people's attention by telling them what they want to hear: they can become property owners with no money down and no qualifying.

Of course, you have to tell prospective co-owners they will be getting only a half interest in the property. You can't mislead people; this will only create problems later. You can be sued or even thrown in jail for fraud if you do that. But you don't want to mention the fact that you're offering only a half interest until you get their interest.

Tell them what they want to hear first and then tell them afterward they get only half interest in the property. Once you have them reading your ad, they are less likely to turn off. If you start the ad by saying, "Half a house for sale," many people won't read any further. Many people just assume they don't want to buy half a house. They want to buy a house outright and so they never learn what you really have to say.

Now, as we said before, many people feel it is a thin line between advertising for home buyers and advertising for prospective tenants. Either way, you are still going to have somebody living in your property and proclaiming himself half owner. You are going to be dependent on that person to make the entire payment. If he doesn't make it, you are going to have to come up with all the money out of your own pocket. If you get into a dispute with your co-owner, you are going to have to get him out of the property; you're going to have to physically remove him and evict him.

ADVERTISING FOR EQUITY-SHARE INVESTORS

You can avoid this by going after an investor instead. Rather than looking for someone who wants to live in the property and is willing to make the entire $800 monthly payment, find someone who has no interest in living in the property. Find an investor who would be willing to pay $200 a month just to be half owner and get half the tax benefits and, presumably, half the future appreciation as well.

You can attract people like this by putting your ad in the "Investment Property for Sale" section or the "Money Wanted" section of your local newspaper rather than the "Homes for Rent" or "Homes for Sale" sections.

> No money down. No qualifying. Half interest in fine
> rental home. Only $200 a month.

Again, the ad is short and to the point and it tells prospective investors what they want to know. They don't have to put up any down-payment money. They don't have to do any qualifying. And it is an investment house you are interested in selling, not an owner-occupied property. And, last of all, you are selling half interest in the property.

This should be less of a problem with investors, since they are not planning to occupy the property anyway and once again, this ad should be enough to get your phone ringing off the wall. The big problem is going to be weeding out the serious investors, finding the people you do want to deal with and getting rid of the ones you don't want to deal with.

CHOOSING AN EQUITY-SHARE PARTNER

You have to establish certain criteria in advance. What are you looking for in an equity-share partner? Why do you want to share the equity with someone else? And what do you expect from that person?

The obvious answer is that you want to share the equity in this case because you want to eliminate the negative cash flow. So what you want is someone who is going to pick up the entire payment and leave you with a property that supports itself rather than a property that drains money from your pocket every month.

So this is the first requirement. You want someone who will make the payment each month. If it is a home buyer or a tenant, you want someone who is capable of paying $800 a month. You must make sure you have someone with a comfortable cushion, say an income of $2,000 to $3,000 a month, someone who can afford those $800-a-month payments.

If you are dealing with an investor, then you want an investor who has more than $200 per month extra, over and above his own normal living expenses. So if someone's living expenses are $1,500 per month, then you want them to have an income of at least $2,000 per month, because in the event of an emergency in his life, or any unexpected expenses, he might be very tempted to divert the money from the house payments.

Secondly, you want somebody with a history of stability, particularly if it is going to be a tenant or a home buyer. You want to know why he is moving. You want to know where he is living now. You want to interview his current landlord. You want to talk to his previous landlord if he had lived at his present address for, say, less than five years. You want to know where he works and how long he has worked there. You want to know everything you can learn about what kind of tenant he has been and what kind of tenant he is likely to be in the future.

What sorts of skills does he have? This is where you get into the secondary considerations. Is it really enough to just eliminate the negative cash flow? Or are you really trying to eliminate maintenance as well? He might be helpless. He might not be able to take care of the property. Do you really want someone who is going to call you every time the faucet or the toilet starts to leak?

HOW LONG WILL YOU SHARE THE EQUITY?

The next point to cover is how long your equity-share agreement is going to run. If you are going to give the co-buyer half the property and half the future appreciation, then at some point he has to be able to cash in that appreciation if he wants to. And you have to be able to cash in your equity in the property if you want to. For this reason, there should be some time limit set on the equity-share agreement. You don't want to be stuck sharing the property with someone else indefinitely. How long do you intend to let the agreement run?

This is completely negotiable between you and your co-owner. Most equity-share agreements run for anywhere from three to ten years, but this is up to you. You can set your equity agreement for a longer period than that or you can let it run for a shorter period. Whatever you and your co-owner—whether it is a tenant, a home buyer, or an investor—agree on will determine how long you hold the property together.

The important thing is, it should be clearly spelled out in the equity-share agreement that the agreement is to last for a specified period of time and that both parties understand this.

FIRST RIGHT OF REFUSAL

The next point you have to cover is what happens at the end of the equity-share agreement. If you are going to be sharing the equity for seven years, for example, what happens when this time period is up? You are going to have three choices. Your co-owner can buy out your half of the equity and choose to keep the property. If you are dealing with a tenant or a home buyer, this is what is quite likely to happen. If that person likes the property and likes living there, he is not going to want to move out at the end of the seven years. He is going to want to go on living in the property and so he should have the right to buy out your equity.

On the other hand, what if he doesn't want to go on living in the property? What if he decides he is tired of living there and wants to move? What if he wants to take his equity and move to another property, or he would like to do something else with his equity? Maybe he is tired of being a property owner. In that case, you would want the right to buy him out, because it is quite possible you might want to keep the property. You might decide the property makes a good rental and there is no reason to give it up just because your equity-share partner has decided he is tired of living there. You might want to buy out his equity in the property and convert the property back to a traditional rental or start a new equity-share agreement with a new tenant or a new home buyer.

Even if your partner is an investor, the two of you may have different priorities. He may still want to keep the property while you may want to get rid of it. Or he may want to dispose of the property and you may want to keep it, so you should also have the right to buy out his equity. You should have first right of refusal. If he decides he doesn't want to keep the property, then you should have the first right to buy out his equity. If neither of you wants to buy out the other one's equity and hold on to the property, then you should agree that the property will be sold and any profit will be split between you.

HOW DO YOU DIVIDE THE EQUITY?

How do you define the profit? How do you define the equity you are going to share? These become particularly important questions if you already have equity in the property at the time you enter into the equity-share agreement. If you start with a property you bought for no money down and you immediately share the ownership, then you haven't got much to lose, because you haven't had any chance to build up any real equity anyway.

But if you start with a property you have owned for a while or a property you bought in a traditional manner, putting down a cash down payment, then you have to consider the difference between present equity and future appreciation and ask yourself which one you are really willing to share. Are you really willing to give up a piece of your existing equity in the property, and if so, what are you going to get for it? Is it necessary to give up that equity, or would you be able to get the same benefits, would you still be able to get someone else to make the entire payment on the property without giving up any of the present equity?

Obviously, this is an important question and it is one you had better answer first, before you draw up your equity-share agreement. For example, if you have a property that is worth $100,000 —for example, if you just bought it for $100,000 with no money down—then the normal way to do things would be to make $100,000 the base price for your equity-share agreement. You would put the tenant on title as half owner and half of any appreciation over and above $100,000 would belong to the tenant. If you wrote up the equity-share agreement to run for five years and the property was worth $120,000 at the end of that time, then you would get $10,000 and your co-owner would get $10,000.

This is all very simple and straightforward. It is the easiest way to write up an equity-share agreement, but it is not the only way and it is definitely not the most desirable way—not from the point of view of the property owner.

As the property owner, your objective is to get rid of your negative cash flow and get rid of your management problems while giving up as little of the future appreciation as you can get away with and giving up absolutely none of any present equity in the property.

How do you do this? By setting your base price higher than $100,000. Just because the property is worth $100,000 and you are going to share equity with someone else, this doesn't mean you have to give him half of any appreciation over and above $100,000. That is completely negotiable. You can set your base price at $110,000 or $120,000 or even $150,000 and reserve the first $10,000 or $20,000 or $50,000 worth of appreciation for yourself as a reward for being the one who went out and found the property and negotiated the original deal. After all, you are doing more work than the other party, so why shouldn't you get more than half of the benefits? There is nothing wrong with this. There is nothing illegal about it. There is nothing immoral about it. You just have to make it clear to your co-owner, whether it is a tenant, a home buyer, or an investor, that he will get half of any future appreciation over and above $110,000 or $120,000 or $150,000 rather than anything over and above the present value of $100,000.

This becomes even more important if you have existing equity in the property. What if the property is worth $100,000, but you have only $80,000 in loans against the property? If you just put your co-owner on title without specifying anything to the contrary in the equity-share agreement, then your co-owner will be entitled to half of the equity over and above the $80,000 in existing loans.

As half owner of the property, he will automatically become half owner of the difference between the existing loans and the present value of the property.

If this is not your intention, you had better spell it out in the equity-share agreement. You had better say that although this person is on title now, his equity interest begins only when the property value reaches $120,000, that anything over and above $120,000 will be split between you and anything under $120,000 will belong to you alone.

This way you make it clear that your agreement is only to share the future appreciation, not to share the present equity in the property. It doesn't matter whether the $20,000 equity comes from cash you put up as a down payment or just from past appreciation. The point is, it is your money; it is your equity. There is no reason why you should have to share it with anyone else.

ASK FOR A DOWN PAYMENT

Of course, you can also ask the prospective co-owner for a down payment. You don't have to put "no money down and no qualifying" in your ad. This is also completely negotiable. You can always put, "low down payment" as opposed to "no down payment." Of course, the more you ask for, the less attractive your ad is going to be.

"No money down" will help to attract co-owners more easily. You have to balance it out. If you are in a market where it is easy to get people to go for an equity-share deal, a seller's market, then don't worry about it. Go for all you can get.

On the other hand, if you are in a buyer's market, you may have to forego a down payment. You may even have to forego holding on to all your present equity and you may even have to share some of it. But don't give away any more than you have to and surely don't give away any more than you intend to.

WHAT IF YOUR CO-OWNER DEFAULTS?

This brings us to another point. What happens if the co-owner defaults on his responsibilities? What happens if he doesn't keep up his payments? Many people worry about the possibility of tenants defaulting like this—and for good reason.

Once you cross the line, once you make the tenant a co-owner of the property, you have blurred the relationship. It is no longer a clear case of landlord and tenant, property owner and renter. Suddenly, you don't have a tenant anymore, you have a co-owner.

So what happens if your co-owner stops paying his rent? You are out $800 a month, that's what happens. Suddenly, you have to come up with $800 a month out of your pocket or the bank, or the mortgage company, or the savings and loan association is going to foreclose on the property.

The lenders don't want to hear that your co-owner was supposed to make the payments and didn't. You took out the loan. You bought the property. You are responsible. Your co-owner may be equally responsible, but all that means is both of you are going to lose the property and both of you are going to have a blot on your credit records.

If you want to avoid this, you have to come up with $800 a month and then you have to find a way to get your co-owner out of the property if he is a tenant or a home buyer. What do you do? You go to court and you try to evict him. But you can't evict him. He goes into court and says, "Your honor, this man is trying to evict me, but I am not a tenant in this property. Here, I have a deed showing that I am half owner of the property. I have just as much right to occupy the property as this other person does. I can evict him as well as he can evict me."

And the judge looks at you and says, "Is this true? Is this person co-owner of the property?"

And you say, "Yes, your honor."

And the judge says, "Case dismissed. There is no grounds for an eviction, because neither one of you is a tenant. You are both co-owners of the property."

Now, put yourself in a position where you have bought the property for no money down. This makes it even worse. There have been cases like this where the judge has turned to the owner of the property, the original owner, and said, "All right. So you are the owner of this property. How much money do you have invested in the property."

And the owner said, "Well, nothing, your honor. I bought the property for no money down because I am a creative investor." And then the judge turned to the tenant or the home owner who was the co-owner of the property and said, "Well, how much money do you have invested in this property?"

And the tenant or the home owner says, "Well, your honor, I have been making payments of eight hundred dollars a month for six months before I finally decided this was silly and I would rather live rent-free."

And the judge looked at the tenant-home owner, he looked at

the original property owner, and he said, "Well now, you sir, don't have anything invested in the property. You bought it for no money down. This person has forty-eight hundred dollars invested in the property. He says he has been making eight-hundred-dollar-a-month payments for six months. I think he has more money invested in the property than you do. Therefore, he has more right to the property than you do. Case dismissed."

You are stuck. You may think you'll foreclose on him if you can't evict him, but you can't foreclose because you are not the lender. The lender can foreclose on both of you, but your only recourse is to take your partner to court and sue him for nonperformance and sue to dissolve the partnership. This could take years. In some areas of the country it could be five years or more before your case is heard and then there are appeals. Not only is this time-consuming, but it is costly and somebody has got to be making those $800-a-month payments while this is winding its way through the courts. Practically speaking, if your cobuyer stops making the payments, you are stuck and you will lose the property unless you can afford to make them on your own.

Some people would say this is a good argument against equity sharing in general, or at least against equity sharing with tenants or home buyers. Some of them will tell you that if you stick to equity sharing with an investor you can't really go wrong.

If you equity-share with an investor, the most you can lose is $200 a month. And you don't have to worry about kicking him out of the property so you can just go on paying the $200 a month, if necessary, while your case drags through the courts and you finally get him off the title. In the meantime, at least you will have a regular tenant in there paying the $600 rent and gradually you will be able to raise the rent until you break even. So the worst that can happen is you will be stuck in your original position of having to put up with $200 a month in negative cash flow. Plus, of course, you will have the expense of trying to sue your co-owner to get him off the title or get him to start performing and paying his $200 a month. But this isn't nearly as bad as being out the entire $800 a month and having a tenant in the property who refuses to pay rent.

Why settle for the lesser of two evils when you can avoid the problem entirely? Equity sharing can be a totally and completely safe way to manage property, if you plan for it in advance.

THE EQUITY-SHARE WRAPAROUND

One easy way to protect yourself is to use what is known as a wraparound loan, or an overriding or all-inclusive mortgage or deed of trust. This makes you a lender who is holding a loan against the property and therefore allows you to foreclose if necessary and get your partner off the title that way.

This is not foolproof, but it is a lot easier than having to take your partner to court and sue him to dissolve the partnership. Let's say you have a property that is worth $100,000 and it has an $80,000 existing first loan. The normal way to equity-share would be to put your co-owner on title, keep the existing $80,000 loan in place, and let your co-owner make all or part of the payments on that loan. Even if you set the base price at $100,000 or higher, you would usually do things this way.

But this leaves you with no protection, as we have already seen. With the wraparound, you do things slightly differently. You keep that $80,000 loan in place, but you write up a new loan to supersede it. You write up a new loan for $100,000 or $120,000 or $150,000, whatever figure you decide on for your base price for your equity-share agreement.

You are the beneficiary on this new loan. You are the lender. The borrowers are yourself and your new co-owner, the partnership that now owns the property. In a sense, you are lending yourself money. You as an individual are loaning $100,000 to you and your co-owner, the partnership. The partnership makes payments to you as an individual on the $100,000 loan. You can set these payments at $800 a month, the same as the payments on the property, including tax and insurance, or you can set them higher. There is no reason why you can't get a positive cash flow. You might get an investor to pay more than $200 a month or get a tenant or a home buyer to pay more than $800 a month. There is no law that says equity sharing means you only get to break even on the property. There is no reason why you can't make money each month and put cash in your pocket.

But the important point is that you hold the first loan on the property. The original first loan becomes the underlying first loan. Your wraparound loan is in first position as far as your co-owner is concerned. The partnership's obligation is to you. The partnership has to make payments on your $100,000 wraparound loan. You, in turn, have to make payments on the underlying $80,000 first loan.

If your partner stops making his payments, whether his payment is $800 a month or $200 a month, it doesn't matter. The partnership is in default on the wraparound loan. As soon as your partner fails to make his payment, you can foreclose. You are now a lender and you can foreclose on your $100,000 wraparound loan. You will still have to keep up the $800-a-month payments on the underlying loans somehow. You will have to come up with the money out of your pocket, whether it is the full $800 a month or just the $200 a month your investor–co-owner is supposed to come up with, but foreclosure is a lot faster and easier than dissolving a partnership.

In some states you can foreclose in as little as thirty days or less. This means that in less than thirty days the partnership— you and your co-owner—loses title to the property. The property either will be sold at auction for $100,000 or more—in which case you will get $100,000 in cash and have to give up only $80,000 to pay off the first loan, so you will be left with a $20,000 profit—or else, more likely, the property will revert to you as the holder of the first loan. If no one bids at least $100,000 for the property at the foreclosure sale, then you will get to take the property as an individual.

The partnership you were part of has lost the title at this point and you as the individual, as the lender who holds the first loan, take the property back. This means you have title by yourself and your co-owner has lost everything in the foreclosure.

This is preferable to trying to take your partner to court, but it is still not the only way or the best way to protect yourself.

THE EQUITY-SHARE PERFORMANCE OPTION

There is a better way still, and we call it the equity-share, or performance, option. And what we do is just combine the option techniques we talked about in the last chapter with the equity-share techniques discussed in this chapter.

Instead of telling the renter, or a home owner, or an investor that we are going to put him on title right away, we tell him he is going to have to work to go on title. He is going to have to perform. During the equity-share period, he is going to have an option to become half owner of the property. In order to exercise that option, he doesn't have to pay us any money, he doesn't have to put up an option fee, but he does have to prove he is going to make his payments each and every month.

It works like this. We tell the prospective co-owner that we are going to put a grant deed—or in some states this would be called a warranty deed—into escrow with an attorney or an escrow or title company. The escrow officer or attorney will be instructed that once the prospective co-owner has successfully made all his payments (we usually use a five-year equity-share agreement, so this means he has to make sixty payments), the grant deed or warranty deed is automatically recorded putting him on title as half owner of the property.

On the other hand, we have him sign a quit claim deed giving up any present or future interest in the property and we give instructions to the attorney or escrow officer, telling him that if the prospective co-owner is more than fifteen days late with any payment—whether this is a tenant-home buyer who is supposed to make the entire payment or an investor who is just supposed to pick up the negative cash flow—the quit claim deed is automaticaly recorded and he loses any chance to become half owner of the property. He reverts to being just a tenant if he is living in the property and if he is an investor, then he just loses any money he has already put up and he loses any future interest in the property. This is clean and simple and clear-cut. If the other person lives up to his part of the agreement, he becomes half owner of the property. If he doesn't, then he doesn't become half owner of the property and we don't lose our equity by dealing with deadbeats. Of course, this also has other advantages. It solves the problem of present and future equity. Ideally, the prospective co-owner doesn't get any equity until he goes on title. This means that for five years, we get all the appreciation. He doesn't start getting appreciation until five years down the road.

Second, we get all the tax benefits during that five-year period. Since we are the ones who are on title, we get all the write-offs. Now again, if you are in a strong buyer's market or a strong tenant's market where there are a lot of properties for rent or a lot of properties for sale, you may have to modify this. You may have to sweeten the pot a little bit to attract co-owners. But when you are in a strong seller's market or a strong landlord's market, you can have it all. You can have the present equity, a good portion of the future equity, and all the tax write-offs for yourself.

Equity sharing can be used in many different ways, and as a landlord you want to make sure you use it to benefit you.

Now, some people say, "Well, this sounds good but it is still not foolproof. What happens if the co-owner makes his payments for five years and then you put him on title and suddenly he stops making the payments? He has made them for five years, but that is no guarantee that he is going to make them in the future." And this is true, but we have even thought of a way around that. There is no reason why you have to go on sharing equity with him at the end of the five-year period. You can write it into the contract that at the end of the five years he goes on title as half owner of the property, but he has to buy out your half of the equity, let you buy out his half of the equity, or agree to sell the property and split the profits. In other words, you don't have to remain on title with him. As soon as he goes on title, you can insist that the property be sold and that way you never have to worry about what happens if he doesn't make his payments. So the equity-share or performance option can be as close to foolproof as any method you are going to find. And then there is one more twist that we haven't even discussed.

EQUITY-SHARE MANAGEMENT

What happens if you share your equity with another investor and neither of you really wants to manage the property? The investor is willing to put up the negative cash flow, but he is not willing or able to do the management.

Why not bring in a third partner and let him manage the property? There is no rule saying you have to split the equity fifty-fifty or that it has to be split two ways. It is your property and so it is up to you to divide the equity in the most desirable way. Keep 50 percent for yourself, give 30 percent or 40 percent to the person who pays the negative cash flow each month and give 10 percent or 20 percent to a third partner who will manage the property.

This way, you can eliminate your negative cash flow and your management problem by having a manager who has got a stake in the property; a manager who considers it an investment in the future rather than just a job.

You will find that equity sharing will allow you to buy properties all over the country, even all over the world, because you will never have to see them. You will never have to deal with them, except when it comes time to collect your positive cash flow and to collect your profit when the properties are sold.

Equity sharing may not cure your rheumatism or your arthritis, but when it comes to real estate problems, particularly management problems, it just may be the solution for the '80s and beyond if only you take the proper precautions and use it right.

Eighteen

Preparing Your Property for Sale

INVESTORS ARE THE WORST BUYERS

Investors are fine to have as friends, acquaintances, clients, and colleagues. They're great to meet at seminars, conventions, and local alumni groups, but they aren't such great people to meet across the bargaining table.

Investors want too much. They know too much. They make too many demands and too few concessions. When it comes down to it, they don't really care if they buy your property or not. If they don't get the price and terms they want, they will walk away and find some other property to buy.

We don't want to deal with people like that. We want to deal with nice, meek home buyers who love our houses and can't wait to move in. Those are the people we want to sell to. They are properly respectful. They don't ask annoying questions about how much we're willing to knock off the asking price, or what kind of special terms we'll give them. They only want to know where to sign their names and whether or not we might possible consider carrying just a small second mortgage.

Home buyers don't always offer us full price, but they never make ridiculously low offers, either. In fact, their hands usually shake if they try to write any number that's more than $5,000 less than the asking price. Besides, the fact is that they *expect* a counteroffer at a high price. They don't really expect to get what they want. All in all, there is no question that home buyers are the best buyers. The only question is how to attract them.

GET THE BEST POSSIBLE DEAL WHEN YOU SELL

The first question a seller probably should ask himself is "Why?" Why do you want to sell the property? The answer to this question will help you determine the *best way* to sell it: through an agent or on your own; "as is" or in prime condition.

Are you selling because you want to? Or are you being forced to sell because you need cash? Are you unhappy with the property itself, or with its location? Will your concerns be likely to plague the new buyer (a freeway right behind the house, small rooms, et cetera) and lower the value, or are they more personal (a boy down the street who hates your son and picks on him; the house is wood frame and you've always wanted a Spanish-style stucco house; you've used up all your depreciation and want property that gives you more tax shelter)?

Your house has three bedrooms, and you live in Berkeley. Three-bedroom houses in Berkeley are selling for as low as $25,000 and as high at $150,000. How high can you realistically price *your* house? It all depends on why you're selling. What can you do to raise the value of the property? The answer is the same. Mostly, it depends on the condition of the property and the location.

Location

Location is widely considered to be the single most important factor in determining the value of any property, because it's the factor hardest to modify or change to suit your own needs. You can knock out walls and make rooms larger, or even repair an inadequate foundation, plumbing, heating, or electrical system much more easily than you can upgrade an entire undesirable neighborhood.

For this reason, location is particularly important when you're trying to decide how much money (if any) to put into your property in order to make it more salable. Ultimately, the location will probably determine the maximum price you can realistically expect to get for your property, no matter how much time, effort, or money you put into improving the property itself. This is not to say that property owners shouldn't keep their property in good repair, or that an investment of time and money in your property won't pay off when you sell. It simply means that the wise seller analyzes his situation carefully before he whips out his checkbook.

The first thing this wise dealer will want to know is how much chance does he have to increase the value of his property at all, and what types of improvements will bring the greatest return on his investment? The only way for the seller to find this out is through a careful analysis of the neighborhood.

What type of neighborhood is it? What type of people live in the area, and why do they live there? Is it by choice, or are they staying there simply because rents and prices are relatively low? Are there mostly families with children, or are there a lot of young singles and/or older retired people in the area? Is the neighborhood relatively stable, or is it gradually or rapidly changing? What are the new people like? Do they have more money on the average then the older, long-term residents, or less? What features are they likely to be looking for in a piece of property, and how much are they willing and able to pay for them?

What Will Improvements Cost?

When you've answered those questions to your own satisfaction, you're ready to get down to specifics: How much will it cost you, the seller, to provide those features that your property doesn't have, and will it be worth your trouble? In other words, will the property really sell faster and for a significantly higher price if you make certain improvements, or will you be wasting time and money that could be better spent in other ways?

One way to make at least a tentative decision is to look around your area, get some idea of the average range of house prices, and then try to decide where your property fits in. If it's closer to the bottom of the price scale, some improvements might be in order; but if it's near the top of the scale, further improvements just might price your house right out of the market and waste your money.

This is the way professional speculators look at a piece of property before deciding whether to buy it and/or fix it up before trying to resell it. It's the only way to ensure that for each dollar you invest, you get back at least a dollar and a half when you sell. And that's the guideline you should use to help you decide whether to improve your property before a sale. If you spend a dollar, it should be worth an extra dollar and a half on the final sale price.

Comparable Prices

You need to know what people in the neighborhood are asking for properties that are comparable to yours. More importantly, what sorts of prices are they actually getting when they sell? (The asking price is virtually meaningless in today's crazy market. It's the actual selling price that counts.)

Why is it so important to know what your neighbors are getting for their properties? Won't improving your property and making it nicer than theirs automatically make the value of your property increase and, therefore, invalidate the comparison? The answer to this question is yes, but only up to a point. Most buyers come into a neighborhood with preformed ideas and prejudices about how much property in that particular neighborhood should cost. Very few people are willing to pay $80,000 for a house in a $50,000 neighborhood, no matter how nice the house is or how much it costs the seller to make it a showplace.

Sure, the house with all the extras will sell faster than nearby houses that aren't as nice, and it will undoubtedly fetch a better price, too—maybe $55,000 or even $60,000 instead of $50,000. But there's no guarantee that the seller will even make back the cost of the improvements, let alone show a profit, because the person with $80,000 to spend would rather spend it in an $80,000 neighborhood (or, preferably, a $90,000 to $100,000 neighborhood), even if he winds up with less house for his money.

We're not trying to discourage anyone from improving his property before he sells. In fact, we'll shortly consider the opposite problem: sellers who lose money by *not* fixing up their property before they sell. But we are urging you to research your own situation carefully so that you wind up spending your money wisely, where it will do the most good. "And where is that?" you ask. "Where can I spend money on my property and be reasonably sure that I will get it back with something extra for my troubles?"

Look around. You've determined that three-bedroom houses in your neighborhood are selling for as much as $75,000, but you've had several realtors come through your house to give you free estimates of value, and the highest any of them would go was $65,000. Obviously, something is wrong. You have a lot of room for improvement—about $10,000 worth of room. Or do you?

Before you panic and call in the contractors, think carefully. Start with your location again. Those $75,000 houses are in your neighborhood, but does that mean that your location is as desirable as theirs? Not necessarily. Possibly those homes have a view, while yours does not. Or possibly your house is on a busy street or corner, which has never bothered *you* but does lower the potential resale value of the property.

But let's say that you've already gone over all these possibilities and decided that your problem is not the location, it's the property. That still doesn't mean that it's time to grab the telephone with one hand and your checkbook with the other; nor does it mean that the agents who gave you estimates were all crazy or incompetent, and that your house is really worth a lot more than they said it was. Possibly those $75,000 three-bedroom houses had two baths, while yours has only one. Possibly they had family rooms or modernized kitchens or some other features that your house doesn't have and which it wouldn't pay for you to add at this point. Then again, there is one more possibility to consider: Perhaps those other houses were in better shape than yours, or perhaps they just made a better impression on prospective buyers.

Spic-and-Span Sells

When is the last time you had your house painted, inside and out? How does the lawn, or yard, look? These things can make a big difference in the selling price—much bigger than most people realize. House buying is often an emotional response. People decide to buy a house because they fall in love with it. Sure, the house has some faults; nothing in this world is perfect. But the buyers aren't looking for the faults; in fact, they're trying to overlook them for the time being, because they don't want anything to spoil the dream. They want to move right in and begin enjoying life; so as long as the price is within reason, they'll pay it without even attempting to haggle. In fact, people in love with a house will often pay even more than the asking price if there are multiple offers, because they don't want someone else to get "their" house.

But a house that's in sloppy, run-down condition, or even one that needs just a paint job, spoils the illusion. The buyers know they can't just move in to the house and live happily ever after. They're going to have a lot of work to do once they move in. Once they realize this, they start to look for other things that have to be corrected, so they'll know exactly what they're getting into. The spell is broken; they're no longer so anxious to buy your house at your price. Now if they buy it at all, they're more than likely to haggle and try to bargain you down on your asking price.

Don't get us wrong; we're certainly not advocating a quick paint and cleanup job to distract buyers and take their attention away from a leaky roof or cracks in the foundation. Willfully concealing or failing to disclose serious defects like that to the buyer is not only unfair and unethical, it's also illegal. If you know problems like this exist and you don't tell the buyer, you leave yourself wide open for a court suit, even if you're selling the house "as is," with no guarantee as to its condition. However, there's nothing wrong with making your house as attractive as possible so that the buyer will want to dwell on the good points rather than the bad ones. To help you determine what can be done to improve your house, and whether it will increase your profit, use the seller's checklist on page 248.

Unfortunately, sometimes a house and/or a neighborhood is so run down that paint and a cleanup won't fool anybody into believing this is their dream house. The only thing that's going to sell it is the price. Somewhere in the world there's a buyer for anything, as long as it's cheap enough, so this is the house that you'll most likely want to sell "as is." But exactly what does "as is" mean, and how do you decide whether or not you want to sell your house that way?

Selling "As Is"

An "as is" sale differs from an ordinary sale in that the seller makes no warranties as to the condition of the property. The buyer agrees to purchase the property in its present condition— however good or bad that may be—and assumes all responsibility for any necessary repairs and improvements. With most sales —those that aren't "as is"—the seller is expected to deliver the property to the buyer in good condition. Even after the buyer takes possession, the seller can still be liable for repairs under certain circumtances. For instance, say the heating system or the stove breaks down a week after the buyers move in, but the repairman says the trouble was building up for a long time before the breakdown. The seller may have to pay damages equal to the cost of the repairs because the heating system wasn't in good condition when the new owners bought the property. With an "as is" sale, the buyers probably wouldn't get any damages unless they could prove that the seller knew about the heating system and had either lied about it or concealed it from the buyers in some other way.

Another important feature of an "as is" sale is that the seller assumes no liability for structural pest-control or "termite" work. This is important to both the seller and the buyer, because termite work is often an expensive proposition. Termite bills of $3,000 to $4,000 aren't uncommon even on seemingly clean, well-maintained houses, particularly those with stucco exteriors. With "fixer-uppers," termite costs often run considerably higher. And unless the owner is carrying the loan himself, it's almost impossible to finance a piece of property (whether it's a house, multiple-apartment units, or a commercial/industrial building) unless a termite report has been done and the lender is sure that the work called for in the report, if any, has been taken care of, or will be within a reasonable period of time after the close of escrow.

No bank or savings and loan association wants to finance a property that may be deteriorating owing to fungus, dry rot, or other problems caused by neglect; and in an "as is" sale the buyer is often required to place money in escrow to cover the cost of these repairs. He can retrieve that money only when he produces a certificate of completion from a licensed structural pest-control company, stating that any necessary work has been completed and the property is clean and structually sound. In a non–"as is" sale, it's usually the seller who agrees to leave the money in escrow (or have the work done himself); the buyer pays only for the cost of the report (generally around fifty to sixty-five dollars).

Termite companies are like all companies; some are more expensive than others. For this reason, a smart seller shops around *before* he puts his property on the market, orders his own termite report, and, if possible, has the work done right away. This way, the seller gets the cheapest price, and prospective buyers are impressed with the fact that they're getting a nice clean piece of property, with all the problems already taken care of. And, again, it keeps buyers from thinking about the property's weaknesses and discovering other problems, not covered in the termite work, that they'll have to deal with at their own expense.

Roofing

Roof work is another matter. Normally the seller isn't considered responsible for the condition of the roof, but it often becomes a negotiable item. Again, a smart seller might have his own roof inspection before he puts the property on the market, and he might even do the work at his own expense, if it's not too expensive and if the property is in fairly good condition aside from the roof.

The roof is one of the first things many buyers think about (or the last thing), so it can sway them one way or the other on a weak sale. If there is roof work to be done, the buyer has to pay it out of his own pocket, and many buyers don't have any money left to spare after paying a down payment and closing costs. It's worth it to these buyers to pay a little more and get a piece of property with no expensive repairs that have to be done right

SELLER'S CHECKLIST					
Feature	Asset	(Neutral) Passable	Deficit	Projected Cost of Improvements	Projected Return
Location					
Style					
Size					
Floorplan					
Grounds					
Paint (Out)					
Paint (In)					
Floors					
Kitchen					
Bathroom(s)					
Attic					
Basement					
Plumbing					
Wiring					
Appliances					
Fixtures					
Foundation					
Roof					
Colors					
Atmosphere					
Decorations					
Furniture					

away. By putting on a new roof before the close of escrow, the seller gets his money back and more. At the same time, he decreases the chances that the buyer will decide to back out of the deal because of unexpected problems at the last minute.

PLAN SALES CAREFULLY

We go to a lot of trouble to make our properties attractive to home buyers and unattractive to investors when we cash out. We do this by putting them in top condition and then asking top dollars, so that there's no profit left for investors. If this sounds selfish, that's because it is.

We've worked hard to build something in this world. We've accumulated many properties, but it hasn't been easy, and we aren't about to sell ourselves short by giving the properties away. We had a game plan when we started buying real estate, and we intend to stick to it. It doesn't include selling properties the way we buy them. We try to buy properties at distress sales from people who need to sell in a hurry and have no choice. We also try very hard to avoid putting ourselves in that situation when we sell. This means plotting everything out beforehand, or at least as much as we can.

The larger your real estate empire, the more planning you have to do. Take our case for an example. We have almost one hundred houses as of this writing, and we're adding more all the time. If we ever tried to sell them all at once, it would be something like a small stock market crash. Anywhere near a hundred houses all put up for sale at once would flood our local market and depress prices.

Therefore, we plan to run our divestiture program in stages. We'll sell off a few houses at a time, and we'll start long before we need to, so that we can maintain maximum flexibility. No one is going to get us with our backs against the wall and start dictating terms and price to us.

STAY FLEXIBLE

As we mentioned before, our basic plan is to hold all our houses for at least five years, but we aren't rigid about that. We're constantly pruning and trimming, getting rid of properties that don't fit into our program. That way we feel comfortable about the properties we do hold. We can hold them indefinitely until the time is right to sell.

That's what this whole book has been building toward. The real purpose of being a landlord is to reap the rewards, one way or another, after years of work. Either you hold on to your properties and keep building a larger and larger positive cash flow machine, or you begin selling, and we intend to eventually sell off most of our properties.

Being a landlord is an honorable and very profitable profession if it's done right. We enjoy it, and it's been good to us. But we also see ourselves doing other things with our lives. We won't get rid of all our properties. We'll hang on to some of them indefinitely, or keep turning them over every five years and acquiring new ones. But eventually we'll get rid of most of our properties. We want the cash and the time to put into new ventures, new challenges. We want to have that cash in our hands instead of keeping it all locked up in our houses. We want to be able to feel it and spend it, to live as rich as we are on paper. Building up the cash flow takes too long. Even with a lot of houses, it takes years. We want to be rich sooner than that. We're impatient.

For those of you who feel the way we do, there are two main alternatives to consider:

1. Work through an agent
2. Sell your property yourself

We're going to examine these choices and look at the advantages and disadvantages of each.

Nineteen

Dealing with Real Estate Agents

If you get suspicious and nervous when you think of dealing with an agent, you can relax. First of all, most agents aren't thieves and swindlers. If anything, they're more honest than the average person because they have their licenses and their business reputations to protect.

Second, even a dishonest agent rarely gets his or her hands on the money when a property is sold. The whole transaction is usually handled by a lawyer or by a title or escrow company that holds all the funds and then disperses them—including the agent's commission—at the close of escrow. Still, even if you aren't afraid of winding up penniless and out on the street, deciding whether or not to list your property with an agent is a big decision. A lot of money is involved, whether you're selling one property or several.

The average real estate commission is from 5 percent to 8 percent of the selling price. This can easily add up to thousands of dollars. Is it worth it? That depends on your situation and your attitude. It's hard for us to comment objectively, since we're licensed agents. Although we don't sell real estate anymore, we view agents from a slightly different perspective than the average person does. We buy many of our houses through agents, and we'll gladly pay commissions to anyone who helps us sell our properties.

AGENTS USE MULTIPLE-LISTINGS SERVICES

An agent will put your property on the Multiple-Listings service. Is this worth the price of the commission? Well, almost every agent we know puts his or her own property on Multiple Listings when he or she is trying to sell it. This means he or she is willing to pay a commission to any other agent who sells the property. Of course, agents in this position pay only half the standard commission, but it's still money out of their pockets. If they didn't feel that they would be getting their money's worth, they wouldn't do it.

Why should agents want to pay someone else to sell their properties when they can sell it themselves? Obviously, they feel they'll get more money for their property that way. It's a simple matter of exposing the property to the maximum number of potential buyers in order to get the best possible price.

It costs the same to put your property on Multiple Listings as it does to list it exclusively with one agent. You pay the same commission that you would pay normally. The Multiple Listings is strictly a fee-splitting arrangement between the agents involved. If one agent lists your property and another agent finds the buyer, the two agents divide the commission.

This arrangement works out well for sellers, too. It makes more properties available to prospective buyers, and it makes more prospective buyers available to bid on properties for sale. This way, everyone gets what he wants. For example, you pick an agent and decide to list your property with him or her. You agree to pay a certain commission if and when the property is sold. He or she then brings buyers to look at the property, but what happens if none of them likes it enough to make an offer? You lose, the agent loses, and the buyers lose. None of you gets what you want.

But just because your agent doesn't have any buyers who want your property doesn't mean it's unsalable. There may be other agents out there who have buyers who would be eager to purchase your property—if they knew about it. Without Multiple Listings, they might never even know that your property is for sale, since they aren't working with the particular agent you've chosen.

Conversely, your agent's buyers don't like your property, but some other agent may have exactly the property they want. Once again, Multiple Listings can be the answer. By agreeing to share the information about their listings—and the sales commissions—the agents involved are increasing their own chances of making sales and earning commissions. More importantly, they are giving your property the maximum exposure it needs to fetch a top-dollar price. If enough people know about your property, you might even get more than one offer and get more than your original asking price.

This is why most agents put their own properties on Multiple Listings. They feel that they'll wind up with a higher *net* sales price—even after paying someone else a commission—than they would get on their own. For example, it's worth paying a $3,000 commission in order to get $5,000 more for your property, isn't it? Why worry about putting $3,000 into someone else's pocket if you're still coming out $2,000 ahead?

Multiple Listings is only one alternative, and attracting buyers for your property is only one of several functions that a good agent should perform. So we're going to look at exactly what's involved when you list your property with an agent; what types of listings are available and exactly what you should and should not expect your agent to do for you; and how to find and evaluate an agent you'll be comfortable working with. Let's start with the various types of listings, because what you should and should not expect your agent to do for you is directly tied to what type of listing you sign.

THE LISTING AGREEMENT

When you list your property, you give one or more agents, or brokers, the right to represent you in the sale of your property. You promise to pay a fee when and if the property is sold. Usually this is a percentage of the sales price, but it can also be a flat fee or a sliding percentage based on the sales price: e.g., 5 percent of the first $50,000 and 6 percent of the balance, or 6 percent of the first $50,000 and 5 percent of the balance, or whatever you and the agent work out; or any excess over and above the minimum return that you want to net. (For example, anything over $60,000 goes to the agent. If the sales price is $60,000 or less, then the agent gets no commission at all.)

OPEN LISTINGS

These are open invitations to agents to sell your property in exchange for an agreed-upon fee, with no obligation on either side. This means you aren't dealing with any one agent exclusively. You're willing to deal with a select group of agents, or with any agent at all who can sell your property.

Open listings are common for large commercial and industrial projects, but they're rarely used when dealing with residential or small income properties. There isn't enough money involved for agents to risk their time and advertising money without a more definite commitment. Instead, many agents will cooperate with owners who are trying to sell properties themselves. The agents will agree to bring buyers to see the property, but they won't advertise the property or represent you, the seller, in any way.

EXCLUSIVE AGENCY LISTINGS

These bind you to working with one agent or company. You still have the right to sell the property yourself, but you can't deal with other agents. Many companies refuse to accept exclusive agency listings. They feel that it's not worth it. Others put restrictions on the seller; e.g., he can't advertise the property at a lower price in his own ads. Or he can advertise only in certain selected media.

Open listings can be open-ended, but exclusive agency listings —like any exclusive listing—must have a definite expiration date. If the property isn't sold by that date, the listing is canceled. It can be renewed at the seller's option, and the law doesn't say what the specific time limit should be, so there's a lot of flexibility in how long you want your property listed.

EXCLUSIVE LISTINGS

These give one agent or company the sole and complete right to sell your property for a fee. Even if you sell it yourself, the agent still gets the agreed-upon commission. He or she has no obligation to share the information about your property—or the commission—with any other agents. If the property is sold during the listing period, the agent you listed it with gets the full commission, period. If he or she agrees to split the commission with any other agent, it's strictly at his or her own discretion.

EXCLUSIVE RIGHT TO SELL—MULTIPLE LISTINGS

This is the most effective way to get your property sold. It gives one agent or company the exclusive right to sell your property. No one else—not even you—can sell it without that agent or real estate company getting their commission. At the same time, this method obligates them to put the information about the property on Multiple Listings and to share the sales commission if another agent brings a buyer.

It's up to you to set the times when other agents can see and show your property, and it's up to your agent to enforce your rules. Putting your property on Multiple Listings does *not* mean letting people come through your house at all hours.

All listings have certain features in common. First of all, commissions are always negotiable, at least in theory. Brokers aren't allowed to get together and set a fixed rate for commissions, but of course they do. It's all done informally. There's no written agreement, but all agents in an area know what the standard commission is—5 percent to 7 percent of the sale price—and they know it's in their interest to maintain that level of payment.

Most agents will make special deals for special clients, but they won't cut their commission for just anyone. If you're selling off many properties at the same time, then by all means try to negotiate a lower commission. The more property you have to sell, the more leverage you have to help you get concessions from agents. But if you have only one or two properties to sell, you should expect to pay the standard fee.

DISCOUNT BROKERS

Of course, there are discount brokers in many areas who work for less than the standard commission. Many of these companies offer good service at a cut-rate price. But there's a serious drawback to dealing with them: you lose the benefits of getting your property on Multiple Listings. Most discount brokers will proudly state that they're members of the local Multiple Listings service, and they put all their properties on Multiple Listings. Unfortunately, this is meaningless, since other agents won't work on listings submitted by discount brokers. The reason for this is simple. Why should an agent work on a property offering a 4 percent or 4½ percent commission when there are plenty of other properties to work on that offer a full 6 percent or 7 percent commission?

This is because of the way the Multiple Listings services work. The buyer's agent and the seller's agent split the commission between them. If the commission is 6 percent, the buyer's agent would get 3 percent. If the total commission is 4 percent, then the buyer's agent would get only 2 percent. Under this type of arrangement, the seller's agent may get a definite advantage from cutting the commission—he gets more business. But there's little or no advantage to the buyer's agent, unless it's such a strong seller's market that agents are desperate to find anything for their buyers. The buyer's agent doesn't increase his business by selling a house listed with a discount broker, he just decreases his income.

THE AGENT MUST WORK FOR HIS/HER MONEY

The other feature that all listings have in common is that they require the agent to use diligence in procuring a buyer. The agent is being paid a fee to perform a service. He or she can't just get your name on the listing contract and then sit back and wait for the property to sell itself. If you get an agent like this, you can cancel the listing at any time, even if the expiration date hasn't come up yet.

Exactly what using diligence to secure a buyer means is a matter of interpretation. Before signing any contracts, you should sit down with the agent and make sure that everything is clearly spelled out so that there will be no misunderstandings later. First of all, let's start with what you can and can't expect from your agent in broad, general terms.

WHAT YOUR AGENT CAN (AND CAN'T) DO FOR YOU

A good listing agent will look out for your interest at all times. He or she will give you suggestions for keeping up or improving your property if you ask for them, will help you make arrangements for any inspections or repairs you have to do as part of the sale, and will even watch your property and take care of it for you if you're gone but still want the property to be shown. Not only that, but the agent will advertise for you, hold the property open for the public and for other agents (with your approval, of course), and once you get a buyer, your agent will stick with you until the escrow closes and you get your money. He or she will see to it that the buyer is qualified for the required loan amount and that the buyer and the buyer's agent are really doing all they can to close the deal smoothly without making any outrageous demands on you.

Even the best of agents can't be expected to get you $70,000 for your $50,000 property just because that's what you want or need to get for the property; tell you what sort of counteroffer a buyer might be willing to accept; get you a satisfactory price on necessary repairs, such as termite work; change the bank's mind if the property doesn't appraise for the purchase price. But, again, a good agent will try.

Now, let's look at some specifics. Exactly what your agent will or won't, should and should not do will vary, depending on the area you live in and your own particular situation. For example, in some areas the agents write up the initial purchase offer, the counteroffer (if any), and the final contract. In other areas attorneys handle this.

The same thing applies once the contract is signed and goes into escrow. In some areas it's the agent's job to work with the escrow or title company, the lenders, and the buyer's agent to see that everything goes smoothly. In other areas, this too is handled by attorneys. You must know what common local practice requires, before you can know what to expect from your agent.

The Agent Handles Advertising

In all cases and all areas, the agent should have primary responsibility for advising you on marketing your property successfully. If you sign a Right to Sell or Exclusive Right to Sell Multiple Listing, the agent and/or the agent's company should bear the full responsibility and cost of all advertising, but there are no set guidelines on what this means. Some companies do a lot of advertising. Others do very little. You should sit down with the agent before you agree to list your property and determine exactly how your property will be advertised.

Some companies run one big newspaper ad containing all their listings. Other companies take out additional ads to spotlight new listings, or run separate individual ads for every property they have for sale. Will your property be advertised on radio or TV? What about magazines or special publications aimed at property buyers or other agents? Newspapers are only one of several possible media that truly creative agents use, and you are entitled to know what your agent intends to do for you and your property.

Ask to see samples of ads the agent has run recently. See if they grab you. Ask to see figures on how effective the ads were. How long was it before the average property sold? Does each ad run every week? How often? Weekends only, or every day? Many companies don't advertise every property every week. They run just enough ads to get calls from interested buyers and then try to peddle their unadvertised listings by direct word of mouth.

HOW MANY OTHER AGENTS DOES YOUR AGENT KNOW?

Find out about the agent's relations with other agents, both inside and outside his own company. This can be extremely important, since agents sell more properties than ads do. Just putting a property on Multiple Listings isn't enough. A good agent goes out of his way to make sure that other agents know about his listings. He'll prepare flyers and distribute them to other offices. He'll attend meetings and gatherings when he has a chance to mingle with other agents and discuss the market and listings for sale. He'll invite other agents and discuss the market and listings for sale. He'll invite other agents to special open-house showings for agents only and then provide them with information sheets about the property, the financing, and other relevant details.

There are many properties in the average Multiple Listings book, so it's natural that there should be competition between sellers and their agents. This is why you need an agent who is aggressive and who is dedicated to marketing your property. Not all agents are good at selling properties or at representing and advising sellers. Some of them are much more comfortable working with buyers. How do you know if someone is a good seller's agent? You ask questions. How many listings have they had in the past year? How many of those sold? How many of their sellers get their asking price or more? How many of their listings sold at market value for the area or higher? What is the agent's overall sales philosophy or strategy? Does he or she prefer representing sellers or buyers? Why?

If this sounds like a lot of work, it is. But think of all the work you've already put in. You spent all that time buying good properties and trying to manage them right, and now it's time to get your real reward. Isn't it worth it to spend just a little more time and get the best possible agent?

LET YOUR AGENT BE YOUR GUIDE

When you finally choose an agent, your financial future is largely going to be in that person's hands. Your agent is going to be your spiritual and financial guide, taking you through the long, difficult process of converting your property to cash. Therefore, the agent should be someone you trust, someone you feel comfortable working closely with.

Your agent should be able to tell you what to do to fix up your house and why; what other houses in the area have been selling for, and what buyers in the area are normally seeking. The agent should be familiar with financing alternatives and be able to advise you on whether or not to hold out for all cash. If you wind up carrying paper, the agent should help set it all up and help you sell the note(s) if that's what you decide to do after the close of escrow. He or she should also advise you on how many properties to sell at once, so that you don't flood the market. It's a big job.

Now that you have some idea of what to look for in an agent, and what to expect the agent to do for you, only one problem is left to solve: finding an agent that fits your needs.

FINDING AN AGENT

This can be as easy or as hard as you want to make it. Buyers and sellers are the lifeblood of any real estate agent's business, so you won't have much trouble getting someone to work with you, especially if you're a seller who's ready to sign a listing. The problem, of course, is getting a *good* agent.

What *is* a good agent? Contrary to popular public opinion, most real estate agents are not crooks. Neither are they hardcore sadists who sit up late into the night dreaming up new ways to saddle the public with leaky roofs and broken water heaters at inflated prices that no one can afford. They're simply hardworking people who are actually a little bit more honest than the general public since agents have to be licensed. The problem isn't so much finding an agent who is honest, or even competent, but finding one that you have confidence in and feel good working with. After all, money's not an issue. Most agents will charge you about the same amount of commission on a listing if you're a seller and, if you're a buyer, you pay nothing anyway. It comes down to which agent you like. The better your relationship with your agent, the harder that person will work for you. In fact, most good agents won't work with people they don't like at all. It's too much trouble. And, especially with buyers, it doesn't pay. The agent usually doesn't make any money. He or she wastes a lot of time, and then the buyer or seller winds up going to another agent, hoping for better results. However, this doesn't mean you have to run out and join country clubs or the local chamber of commerce just to meet real estate agents. There are other ways.

Open Houses

Every Saturday and Sunday you see signs on street corners advertising properties, mostly houses, that are open for inspection. Open houses are an excellent way for buyers and sellers to see what's on the market and what sells and what doesn't. They also provide an excellent way to meet real estate agents (or owners, if you prefer to do it that way). Go in, walk around, and see what happens. Is the agent friendly, helpful? How do agents react when you explain that you're just looking around and aren't a serious buyer? Try to watch the different agents as they talk to other people (particularly if you are a seller), and see which ones you like from that perspective. Take notes, and then go back and contact the agent that you liked best.

Go to as many open houses as you need to until you find the agent that you feel is right for you. Just make sure that you let all the agents know what you're doing, so they don't spend time with you that they could be spending with someone who is ready to buy or sell right away. Courtesies like that will be appreciated by the kind of agent you want to find, and can tell you a lot about the kind you don't want when you watch their reactions.

Newspaper Ads

These also appear every Saturday, and sometimes during the week. They're another excellent way to survey the market and meet agents—over the phone, anyway. They also give the smart buyer or seller a chance to assess the various companies around. Study the ads for a couple of weeks, and see if any one company's ads are consistently appealing to you, and then contact that company by phoning them or going to their office.

The one drawback to this method is that it won't tell you much about an individual agent. It will only inform you about the company that he or she works for. However, knowing something about the company is some help, because quite often company policy has a large effect, for better or worse, on the conduct of the individual agents within that company, their behavior toward clients, and their level of integrity. But individual personalities count for a lot, too.

For example, Dave Chodack's company has two offices and employs about thirty agents. The owners are selective; not just anyone is hired. No matter which of their agents you deal with, that person will be honest, competent, conscientious, and willing to work hard for you. But there similarities cease, because these agents are thirty very individualistic people, ranging in ages from twenty-two to over sixty, with all the personality differences that you would expect in such a diverse group. Which of these agents would be best for you depends on your individual personality, and each individual agent is likely to give you a very different impression of what Red Oak Realty is like. There's really no way you can determine this through newspaper ads, unless you are consistently attracted to the ones with the same agent's name in them, so you have to play it by ear and take your chances. After you've interviewed a few agents and worked with two or three, you'll develop your own instincts for choosing agents who suit you.

HOW NOT TO CHOOSE AN AGENT

Many people just walk into the closest, or best known, or most attractive-looking real estate office in their area, and say that they want to buy or sell some property. Some sellers will call several real estate companies to come out and evaluate their property, and then list with the company that gives them the highest estimate of the property's value. Many buyers will give their names to several different agents, figuring that whoever finds them the right property first will get the commission and, therefore, the agents will all work harder trying to compete with each other.

In our minds, none of these methods is very good, because none involves choosing an individual agent on the basis of how well that agent's personality fits yours. That's not to say that you and your agent have to fall madly in love at first sight and become best friends forever after; but, ideally, you'll be working closely together, so the relationship should be as comfortable as possible and be based on mutual trust.

Listing with the company that gives you the highest estimate of value often sets you up for disappointment. Agents know that sellers sometimes choose this way, and so they'll often give deliberately high estimates just to get the listing. But even if they're sincere, agents aren't perfect. They make mistakes, like anyone else. Ask ten agents to appraise your property, and you'll probably get at least four or five different estimates.

As for the idea that agents will work harder for a buyer who's working with several agents, all we can say is "No way." Any experienced agent who knows that a buyer is also working with other agents will immediately put that buyer at the bottom of his or her client list. The agent will call that buyer about any given property only after all the "good" clients, the loyal ones, have had a chance to turn it down. This leaves the multiple-agent buyer with the scrapings from the bottoms of everybody's barrel, so this person rarely hears about any of the really good buys on the market.

Now that you know what to expect from real estate agents, let's take a look at selling your property without an agent.

Twenty

Selling Property Yourself

Once you've figured all the expenses and prepared the property for sale, the next thing you have to worry about is advertising. If you list the property, this is the agent's responsibility, but when you're on your own, you're the one who has to come up with ads that will attract buyers.

KEEP YOUR ADS BRIEF BUT EFFECTIVE

Think about it. By this point, you should have completed a full evaluation of your property. You should be well aware of its strengths and weaknesses. Forget the weaknesses and concentrate on the good features. Those are what potential buyers are looking for. Pick the strongest, most attractive features your property has to offer and mention them in your ads. Put yourself in the buyer's place and imagine what you'd want to know if you were looking for a new home. Wouldn't you be most interested in the location, the price, and the special features?

Where is the house? People—especially home buyers—start with an area they want to live in, and then choose a house there. Investors will look at a house in any area, if the price and terms are right, but home buyers usually want a specific area.

Home buyers also want specific features, the more the better. Does your house have wall-to-wall carpeting? Central air-conditioning? A large backyard, extra bathrooms, or a modern kitchen? Mention these in your ad, but don't feel as if you have to get everything in at once. Remember, the ad is costing you money, and you're probably paying by either the word or the space. Either way, you want to keep your ad as brief as possible. The buyer doesn't want to wade through extra information any more than you want to pay for it. Put in just what you need to and nothing more.

Abbreviate whenever you can. For instance, three bedrooms and two baths can easily become "3BR, 2BA" with no real loss of meaning or understanding. On the other hand, "Qt. st. pnt. nghb." can be very confusing, so you're better off spelling it out as "quiet st., pleasant neighborhood." Watch realtors' ads to see how they do it. They're professionals, and they know the little key phrases that draw buyers. Pick up all the pointers you can from them, and remember that your main audience is likely to be women.

Women buy houses. More and more single women are buying their own homes, but more importantly, it's usually the woman who chooses the home for the family. There are definite exceptions, but in the majority of cases, if the husband likes the house and the wife doesn't, they won't buy the house. If the wife really likes the house, they'll probably buy it even if the husband isn't crazy about it.

Women spend more time in the house and they spend more time thinking about the house. This is true even in this age of working wives. It's a fact of life, and it should influence your sales pitch. Are women going to get excited because the house has copper plumbing? It's hard to imagine a woman forcing her husband to call about your ad, jumping up and screaming, "Oh George! We've just got to go see this place. It's got a new roof and a fresh cap on the foundation!"

EMOTIONS SELL HOUSES

Those things may become important later. After all, they can save buyers a lot of money. But they aren't the features you want to put in your ad. "New stove and refrigerator," or "view in three directions" are the things you want to stress. Grab buyers by their emotions first and worry about their rational minds later. Investors buy rationally. Home buyers buy emotionally, which is why they'll pay more for the same house, and why they're the buyers you want to attract. So offer home buyers features they can see and enjoy and appreciate. That's what they'll pay for. Spacious, modern kitchens and baths, built-in appliances, decks, and automatic sprinkler systems are the things they dream of—not brand-new sewer lines or septic tanks.

Buyers also look for help with financing. If you were using an agent, that would be part of his or her job. When you aren't using an agent, it's up to you to contact lenders and find out what financing is available. You must be able to evaluate different loan programs and decide which ones have the best rates and terms so that you can show prospective buyers the best way to buy your property. You then have to make sure your buyers complete all their paperwork correctly and submit it to the lender. You can't really relax until the close of escrow.

COOPERATING WITH AGENTS

Of course, if you aren't a stubborn purist, you can compromise. You can work with agents even though you decide not to list your property. You can agree to pay a full or partial commission, since the agents will represent only the buyer and you will represent yourself to any agent who brings you a buyer. This way, you can have all your bases covered in case selling the property is harder than you had anticipated.

If you decide to do this, you should make up some flyers and distribute them to real estate offices in your area. Give the address of the property, a description, the asking price, and information about financing, terms, and other details. Also state the fee you will pay to the agent who brings you a buyer.

Another good trick to know is that in many areas, the local board of Realtors organizes a weekly tour of new listings for its members. Find out when this tour is, and then arrange to hold your property open at that time and add it to the tour. It never hurts to mention that refreshments will be served and/or a door prize given away. This may sound hokey, but it works because it gets agents to come to your open house. Once inside, one of them may decide your house is exactly what one of his buyers is looking for. And even if you don't get immediate results, at least the local agents have some reason to remember that your house is available and what it's like the next time a buyer does want this kind of property.

Of course, it's your responsibility to clear all this traffic with the tenants, but that would also apply if you were to list the property. Part of being a successful landlord is preparing your tenants for the idea that the property will eventually be sold. You don't need hostile tenants hanging around when you're showing the house.

If necessary, you can always evict uncooperative tenants. This is a last resort, though, because it's unpleasant and afterward you're left with a vacant property that's producing no income and costing you money until it's sold. This is something you want to avoid if possible. If you treat your tenants fairly and manage them right, you shouldn't have any real trouble with them when it's time to sell. That way, your only remaining problem should be deciding whether to cash out or to carry some paper, which is the difference between taking all your profit in one lump sum or acting like a banker.

Afterword: Now, Go Out and Do It!

In this book, we've tried to show you how to make money in a businesslike and ethical way. Being a landlord doesn't meant you have to love your tenants, but it does mean you have to treat them fairly and honestly. This is not just common courtesy; it's common sense. Slumlords go for the quick buck and sometimes they get it, but they don't make much money in the long run, because their tenants and/or the local authorities usually drive them out of business sooner or later and when this doesn't happen, then they lose money when their properties reach the point of deterioration beyond repair.

As a landlord your chief assets are your properties and your tenants. You don't want to abuse and mistreat either one of them or take them for granted. But nor do you want them mistreating or abusing you, and this means you must choose both your properties and your tenants carefully.

You have to buy right to own right, manage right, and ultimately sell right. That is the overall theme of this book. You don't want to buy just any property any more than you want to rent to just any person. You're planning your future every time you look at a property or interview a tenant, so it's worth putting a little thought, time, and effort into it beforehand, to be sure what you're looking for. Set your standards high—as long as they're not downright unrealistic—and then stick to them.

This book is meant to be a road map to guide you along the way to financial independence. It's not a get-rich-quick scheme.

It took us four years of work and sweat and planning and reading books like this and going to seminars, before we achieved our goal. It wasn't always easy, but it was exciting. It was easily the most challenging thing either of us has ever done. Of course, what really made it all worthwhile is the money, buckets and buckets of money. No, we didn't become instant, overnight millionaires, but we did finally make it and that's what counts.

We started with nothing, with less than nothing if you count all our debts. Now, four years later, we're millionaires. We do what we want when we want and we're not even tied down by our properties anymore, because we have our program on automatic pilot. We no longer have to be around to make it work.

We didn't do all of this through luck, or any innate genius for business and real estate. We learned from trial and error and by listening to those people who could teach us something and help our program grow and prosper. And in the past couple of years, we have helped many others get started too.

If you follow the plan we lay out in this book, we know it will work for you, just as it did for us. Before you know it, you will be living out your dreams, too. Good luck to you. We're waiting to hear your success story.

—Mike and Irene Milin

Index

About the Authors

Mike and Irene Milin are the world's most successful couple in real estate education, the "Dynamic Duo" whose seminars in real estate management have shown thousands across the country how to find, purchase, and rent properties. Only a few years ago, the Milins were plagued by debt and unemployment, but by studying the ways other entrepreneurs had made fortunes in real estate, the Milins developed the sure-fire "Milin Method" and became millionaires almost overnight. In the past two years, they have traveled more than 500,000 miles coast to coast showing investor groups how they achieved their goals with hard work and a savvy program that gets results. The Milins live in Tucson, Arizona.